MIDLAND RED
SINGLE-DECKERS

DAVID HARVEY

AMBERLEY

Front cover above: **1265, HA 6194**
The SOS IM4s of 1931 still retained the idiosyncratic appearance of the buses built by Midland Red in the late 1920s and followed the company policy of a lightweight body coupled to a fairly powerful petrol engine. The narrow cab and offset radiator, the high skirt level of the body panels, the unmatched pair of front wings, the petrol tank under the driver's seat and a total lack of destination box were all features of this model, yet it was as up to date with its specification as contemporary models built by the large commercial manufacturers. 1265, (HA 6194), with its Short Brothers B34F body, stands on the waste-ground used as a parking area in front of Digbeth Garage in Birmingham on 21 August 1949. Behind it is a 1938 SOS SON, 2211, (EHA 779), with an English Electric B38F body. (D. Tee)

Front cover below: **2415, GHA 334**
Not quite what it seems! The well-known bus and railway photographer Les Perkins was called up into the RAF and had to report for duty at a training station in Gloucestershire. He took his wife, Winnie, and their family on a Midland Red bus – the almost brand new 2415, (GHA 334), an SOS SON with a Brush B38F body – to the nearest point to the station, along with a number of other recruits and their families. 2415 is fully painted-out with white wartime markings and masked headlights. The last photograph Les took of his wife before beginning his war service was of her standing on the step of the bus parked outside the Plough Hotel, Quedgeley, on 26 May 1940. (L. W. Perkins)

Rear cover: **3942, OHA 942 and 3718, NHA 718**
Midland Red was among the pioneers of underfloor-engined single-deckers and between 1946 and 1952 built up a large fleet of chassis with bus bodies built by either Brush or Metro-Cammell. The exceptions were the BMMO S13s, some of which, such as 3942, (OHA 942), had Brush DP40F bodywork and could be distinguished by their black roofs. They were the only dual-purpose single-deckers in the fleet from 1952, until the later integral S15 entered service in 1957. 3942 is working on the 310 route from Worcester to Cleobury Mortimer. Alongside it, 3718, (NHA 718), is parked at the bus shelter in Worcester Bus Station, about to work the 312 service to Lickhill via Stourport. Lickhill is to the north-west of the Severnside canal town of Stourport. (D. John)

First published 2017

Amberley Publishing
The Hill, Stroud
Gloucestershire, GL5 4EP

www.amberley-books.com

Copyright © David Harvey 2017

The right of David Harvey to be identified as the Author
of this work has been asserted in accordance with the
Copyright, Designs and Patents Act 1988.

British Library Cataloguing in Publication Data.
A catalogue record for this book is available from the British Library.

ISBN 978 1 4456 6796 6 (print)
ISBN 978 1 4456 6797 3 (ebook)

Typeset in 10pt on 13pt Sabon.
Typesetting and Origination by Amberley Publishing.
Printed in the UK.

Contents

Acknowledgements

The author is grateful to the many photographers acknowledged in the text who have contributed to this volume. I wish to thank all of those who are still alive for allowing me to use pictures, many of which were taken more than sixty years ago. Thanks are also due to the late Roy Marshall, Les Mason and Peter Yeomans, who all printed photographs for me many years ago and generously gave permission for me to use their material. Where the photographer is not known, the photographs are credited to my own collection. Special thanks are due to my wife Diana for her splendid proofreading.

The book would not have been possible without the continued encouragement given by Connor Stait at Amberley Publishing.

1902–1911: The Pioneering Early Years

The Birmingham & Midland Motor Omnibus Company (BMMO) began to operate motor buses in the Birmingham and Black Country area on 25 May 1912. The first buses were all petrol-electric Tilling-Stevens TTA1 and TTA2 double-deckers, but from 1913 until 1922 all purchases were single-deck. By early October 1914, the first thirty of the original double-decker fleet had been sold to Birmingham Corporation Tramways when the famous 'Birmingham Agreement' came into effect, leaving the company with just seven double-deckers. The Corporation now had the rights to operate their own buses within the Birmingham boundary, while BMMO could radiate its services from Birmingham initially into the nearby Black Country, later taking on routes in Worcester, Tamworth and Kidderminster not long after the outbreak of the First World War. The vehicular needs of the company were increasingly becoming for single-deck buses.

Tilling–Stevens, TTA1, TTA2 and TS3 Single–Deckers

The buses purchased from 1914 and throughout the First World War were Maidstone-built Tilling-Stevens TS3 petrol-electrics, but these normal-control buses were nearly all single-deckers. These buses were available to bus operators around the country during the First World War because their petrol-electric transmission was considered by the British Army to be too complicated to maintain in the battle areas in France and Belgium. Elsewhere, AEC and Daimler buses were commandeered by the War Department as they had gearboxes and clutches, but the Tilling-Stevens BMMO single-deck fleet had petrol engines driving a generator; this provides traction current to an electric motor, which drove the bus. This is basically the same principle as a modern diesel-electric railway locomotive. Ironically, despite the Army's alleged aversion to their petrol-electric transmission, it enabled trainee drivers to learn to drive them much more quickly as they dispensed with struggling with a clutch and crash gearbox!

In 1913, 8–13, (O 9937–9942), were delivered with Birch B27R bodywork in 1913, thus becoming BMMO's first single-deckers. These were Tilling-Stevens TTA2s with Birch B27R bodywork and were immediately followed by 14–19, (OA 343–348), which were the last TTA2s delivered to BMMO and had B27R bodies built by the London-based coachbuilder Hora.

The first large orders for single-deck buses came after the agreement with Birmingham Corporation Tramways, which came into effect on 5 October 1914. After this the need for double-deck buses was dramatically reduced, as Midland Red began their rapid expansion beyond the city boundary. As a consequence, there were several groups of Tilling-Steven's new TS3 chassis delivered throughout the First World War. They had a 14 ft 6¼ inch wheelbase and were powered by a pair-cast four-cylinder 4.355-litre engine rated at 40 hp. These wartime single-deckers buses delivered to Midland Red had a myriad of different manufacturers' bodywork mounted on the new Tilling-Stevens chassis. The buses were all built with lightweight bodies capable of seating between twenty-nine and thirty-two passengers and were a great success, therefore allowing the company to expand their operating area dramatically by about 1920. Between 1914 and 1922 some 233 Tilling-Stevens TS3s were placed in service. Bodies were built by Tilling – including 21–50, (OA 4550–4579), and 51–60, (OA 7080–7089), in 1914 and 1915 respectively, Brush, 61–70, (OA 7090–7099), 74, (OA 7103), 75–101/103–118, (OE 1104–30/32–1147), 119–126, (OE 3148–3153) – with thirty-eight being built by Strachan and, unusually, some forty-three by Birmingham Railway Carriage & Wagon, the Smethwick-based railway carriage-builder who was dabbling in building bus bodies for the first time.

At the end of the First World War, BMMO acquired a number of Tilling-Stevens chassis via the War Department and, with canvas tilt lorry bodies, they were temporarily placed in service to cover for the awaited new vehicles. They lasted barely two years before being withdrawn.

THE FOUNTAIN, EDGBASTON.

251

Standing in Hagley Road at the junction with Sandon Road is 251, the police licence number given before the introduction of registration numbers. This single-decker was a 12 hp Napier-engined Mulliner and had a B10F body with extra capacity for another two standing passengers. It ran on the service between the Sandon Road fountain and New Street. The fountain itself was dismantled during the First World War. Although unreliable, the Mulliner was used for several months on this route, but was never given a registration under the terms of the 1903 Motor Car Act, which was enacted on 1 January 1904. (Commercial Postcard)

O 9938

Almost all of the buses operated by the predecessors of the Birmingham & Midland Motor Omnibus Company and the company itself were double-deckers. After the agreement was made with Birmingham Corporation, which came into effect on 5 October 1914, only single-deckers were purchased for the next eight years. Parked in front of the main office of BMMO in Bearwood Road is O 9938, which was one of the first of these single-deckers. This Tilling-Stevens TTA2 had a Birch B27R body. The six earliest new Midland Red acquisitions were built in 1913 and were the only ones built with rear entrances that were ever operated from new by the company. O 9938 was fitted with a Birch O18/16RO body in 1919 and was re-registered O 7100. The single-decker is equipped with a luggage rack and is carrying boxes of goods for delivery, while on the waist rail is a slip board reading 'NEWS OF THE WORLD SPECIAL'. The bus is presumably being used as a replacement for the Birmingham & Midland Tramways parcels service to Lionel Street at the edge of Birmingham's city centre. (BMMO)

O 9940

In November 1914 the newly formed BMMO Company took over the former Worcestershire Motor Transport Company routes in the Kidderminster area after their six single-deckers were commandeered by the War Department. Midland Red had opened their new route between Birmingham and Kidderminster in April 1914 and the newly acquired services included the Kidderminster to Bewdley route. O 9940 was one of the six Tilling-Stevens TTA2s with Birch B27R bodywork and had a deep, straight-sided radiator. O 9940 stands in Bewdley when working on the recently numbered 43 route, and is seen with its crew posing alongside their bus. (D. R. Harvey Collection)

OA 343

OA 343 stands in the bodybuilder's yard when new in 1913. One of six buses in the class, this Tilling-Stevens TTA2 had a Hora twenty-seven-seater body, but, for the first time in the Midland Red fleet, this bus had a front entrance. Hora were based in Camberwell in London and were in business until the 1920s. The bus remained in service, albeit with a second-hand body, until 1925. (D. R. Harvey Collection)

OA 4552

Hardly recognisable today, Five Ways marked the end of Broad Street. Crossing the tram tracks from Islington Row into Ladywood Road is OA 4552, a Tilling-Stevens TS3 dating from 1914. It was one of thirty vehicles delivered just prior to the outbreak of the First World War. It originally had a Tilling B29F body and, amazingly, was rebodied four times with similarly styled bodies before finally being withdrawn in 1928. The statue dominating the junction between Hagley Road on the right and Calthorpe Road on the left was erected in 1859 to the memory of Joseph Sturge (1793–1859), who was a Quaker, a grain importer and a leading campaigner for the abolition of slavery. (Commercial Postcard)

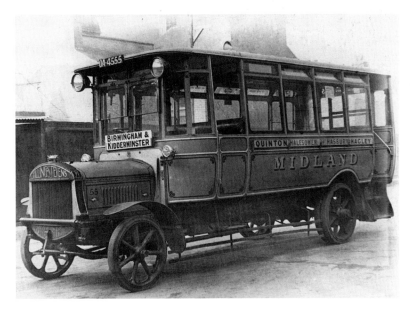

OA 4555

OA 4555 is parked in Carlyle Road Works in 1920 prior to being rebodied with a Birch B29R body. This Tilling-Stevens TS3 dated from 1914, when it had a Tilling B29F body, and was fitted with a pair of roof-mounted headlights. It was eventually withdrawn in 1926. The bus had been working on the number 26 route, which operated between Birmingham and Kidderminster via Quinton, Mucklow Hill and Halesowen, Hasbury and Hagley. (BMMO via B. Baker Collection)

OA 4566

During the First World War, a number of Tilling-Stevens TS3 buses were converted to run on coal gas. This was carried in a large gas balloon that was mounted on the route. OA 4566 was allocated to Tamworth Garage and is seen operating on the number 63 route between Tamworth and Atherstone in 1917. It was fitted with headlights in the normal mudguard position. The Tilling B29F body was the standard 1 type and entered service in 1914. It was rebodied twice, first in 1919 and then in 1921 and was withdrawn in 1927. (D. R. Harvey Collection)

OA 4571

Tilling-Stevens TS3 OA 4571 stands in the High Street of Henley-in-Arden in front of one of the many hotels in the village. The High Street is about one mile long and contains a delightful mixture of half-timbered fifteenth-century and Georgian stone or brick-built properties. OA 4571 was reputedly on the inaugural run of the service in 1914 and is shown on a return trip from Stratford-upon-Avon to Birmingham. This bus had a Tilling B29F body and was virtually brand new. After being rebodied, the bus would stay in service until 1927. (D. R. Harvey Collection)

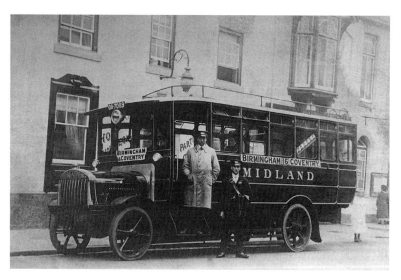

OA 7089

Tilling-bodied OA 7089 was a Tilling-Stevens TS3 petrol-electric and was the last of a batch of ten such single-deckers purchased in 1915. It has the slightly later fencer's mask radiator and, after receiving another similar body in 1921, was taken out of service in 1928. It is working on the newly numbered 16 route from Birmingham to Coventry. The crew stand at the front entrance as it waits in Coventry before resuming its duty. These single-decker buses had a capacity for only twenty-nine passengers and were replaced in 1923 on busy services such as this by the SOS FS fifty-one-seater double-deckers. (D. R. Harvey Collection)

OA 7103

OA 7103 was the usual Tilling-Stevens TS3 petrol-electric, which had become the standard chassis for BMMO. It entered service in 1916 at a time when other bus operators had already had buses commandeered by the War Department. The complicated system of the petrol engine driving an electric dynamo, which then drove the prop shaft, meant that the Tilling-Stevens petrol-electric model was rejected for war service by the military, and that BMMO could continue to obtain this type of bus. This bus was the first ever with a Brush body and had a B29F layout. (R. Marshall Collection)

OB 1104

When being used on the Birmingham to Bromsgrove route, OB 1104 was hit by an oncoming lorry, whereupon it received noticeable damage to the offside of the driver's cab. After the accident, the bus crew and the Midland Red recovery crew pose in front of the 1916 Brush-bodied Tilling-Stevens TS3 bus, while behind is the lorry, which looks as if it might have come off second best. The lorry driver and owner stand alongside the menacing figure of a member of the local constabulary. (D. R. Harvey Collection)

OE 1135

Standing in the town square in Banbury is OE 1135. This 1919-built Tilling-Stevens TS3 petrol-electric had a Brush B29F body and was taken out of service in 1928. The crew of the bus pose in front of their charge, which is working on the service to Chipping Norton along what would later become the A361. It was typical of the sort of rural bus services that these early Tilling-Stevens TS3s were frequently employed on. Even if the ride on indifferent road services on rubber tyres was jarring, and despite running at the legal top speed of 20 mph, the bus was able to link the larger market towns with the smaller towns, such as Chipping Norton, as well as the outlying villages. (P. Kingston)

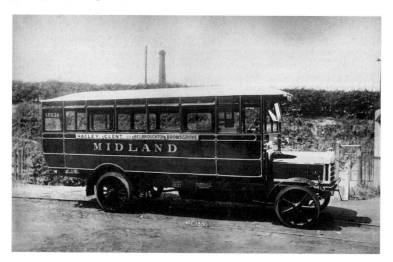

OE 1137

Positively gleaming in the sunshine in Loughborough is OE 1137. This Tilling-Stevens TS3 petrol-electric has the Brush 2 type five-bay construction body, which was fitted with wooden window frames, making the glass less prone to breaking. The bodywork contained seating for twenty-nine passengers and has a slip board for what later became the number 318 route from Stourbridge to Bromsgrove, via a tour through the Clent Hill by way of Hagley, Clent village, Belbroughton and Catshill. OE 1137 was rebodied with a similar structure in 1922 and was scrapped in 1929, by which time it would have been converted to run on pneumatic tyres. (BMMO)

OH 1232

OH 1232 receives some attention to its engine outside the refreshment stop at the Rising Sun Hotel between Mold and St Asaph in about 1921. It is working on the number 201 long-distance service from Birmingham to Llandudno via Wolverhampton, Wellington, Shrewsbury, Wrexham, Rhyl and Colwyn Bay. Such buses used on these long services were equipped with cushioned seat squabs, which at least softened the harshness of the eight-hour-plus journey! (G. Davies)

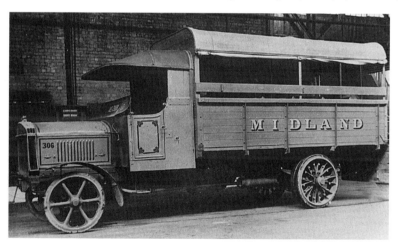

OE 7306

Thirty-nine Tilling-Stevens TS3 lorries were purchased from the War Department in 1920 as an emergency measure. These were pressed into service with a refurbished canvas tilt lorry body that was fitted out with steps at the rear. The vehicle is registered OE 7306, but was temporarily about to be registered OE 3153, which was chalked on the bulkhead and on the chassis frame just above the silencer on the exhaust pipe. The desperate need for buses meant that this lorry-bus was pressed into service during 1929, prior to it being rebodied by Birmingham RC&W with a B29F body adapted to the long 15-foot wheelbase of these ex-War Department lorries. The tilt van body was not used again. In this rebodied state, OE 3153 would stay in service until 1930. (D. R. Harvey Collection)

1922–1928: The First Generation
of SOS Buses

The pioneering work of the Birmingham & Midland Motor Omnibus Company (BMMO), better known as Midland Red, in the development of both double- and single-deck buses in this country is well known. The pre-Second World War work of L. G. Wyndham Shire, the Chief Engineer appointed by the fledgling bus operator in April 1912, was the driving force behind keeping the company at the vanguard of forward-thinking design.

Throughout the 1920s, Midland Red buses were responsible for the closure of many tramway systems, especially in the Black Country, due to their relative speed and comfort in relation to the old, Edwardian tramcars they were competing against. Up to 1922, the standard Midland Red bus had been a petrol-electric chassis built by Tilling-Stevens of Maidstone but these were too slow and were very poor on hilly routes. They were being outperformed by small independent operator's buses, especially in the Black Country, Worcester and North Warwickshire. The company purchased a pair of eleven-seater Model T Fords in 1921, while during the following year fourteen 20 hp Garfords imported from the USA were purchased with a variety of bodies ranging from fifteen to twenty-four seats. Mr Shire's report, after extensive testing, was that the company should build its own buses to his specification, which could consolidate services, expand the area of operation and drive the associated BET tramway operators into extinction

An important by-product of the decision to manufacture their own buses at Carlyle Road Works was that the company had the capacity to manufacture buses for other BET Group operators, of which nearly a thousand were supplied. Thus, the SOS marque was born, with the letters standing for 'Shire's Own Specification'.

SOS S Type

The first bus built by Midland Red to have the SOS name marque was the forward-control S type. Shire's original design was a straight-framed, lightweight, normal-control chassis fitted with a four-cylinder side-valve 4.344-litre petrol engine with Ricardo modified cylinder heads, a four-speed gearbox and the early use of pneumatic tyres. The new chassis was a development of the final batch of Tilling-Stevens TS3s delivered in 1922, which by that time were being built with four-speed gearboxes. The first of the SOS S types actually had Tilling-Stevens TS3 chassis frames. The chassis was fitted with a radiator similar to those on the Tilling-Stevens buses but the SOS version was taller, straight-sided and had the legend 'MIDLAND RED' on the header tank. The bus chassis version was usually fitted with a thirty-two-seat, wooden-framed, six-bay body built by Brush of Loughborough and an all-up weight of 3¾ tons. The result was a neat, fast, reliable and lightweight normal-control single-decker (albeit with only rear wheel brakes), with a better than average seating capacity, which did everything to meet the company requirements. By 1925 some 205 had been built, with 113 being used by BMMO. *(From this point the buses will be referred to by their A numbers as well as their registration marks for ease of identification.)*

The first year of production was 1923 and the first twenty-two SOS S types were all delivered to Midland Red. The first SOS S type was 346, (HA 2330), which was quickly followed by 347, (HA 2333). The SOS S type was built in both bus and canvas-topped charabanc form, with all deliveries to BMMO until the end of 1924 having the bus bodies built by Brush and the charabancs by Davidson, a Manchester coachbuilder. The deliveries of both types of SOS S were intermingled, but the vehicles bodied as buses are as follows:

A Number	Registration Number	Body and Capacity	Year New
Nos 349–356 (ex–TSM TS3)	HA 2334–2343	Brush B32F	1923
No. 361 (ex–TSM TS3)	HA 2345	Brush B32F	1923
Nos 364–365/368 (ex–TSM TS3)	HA 2347/4/6	Brush B32F	1923
Nos 395–6/400–405 (ex–TSM TS3)	HA 2359/65–73	Brush B32F	1924
Nos 410–416 (ex–TSM TS3)	HA 2360–2/4/3/82	Brush B32F	1924
Nos 426–427/29–33/5/8/40–44/7/54–6 (ex–TSM TS3)	HA 2375–6/8/4/7/9–80/4/3/6/5/7/90/81/92/89/8/91	Brush B32F	1924
Nos 457–68/70/5–7/81/4/8–9/505/7–12/29/41/8/50/7/9/65–6/8/70–1	HA 2393–6/9/7–8/2401/0/2–06/10/07–9/11–2/41/3/5/4/6–8/65/76/82/4/93/5/3502–5/6/7–8	Carlyle B32F	1925
Nos 469/71–4/8/80/2–3/5–6/91–8/501/3–4/6/13–822/4–8/30–7/9–40/2/4	HA 2419/20–1/18/29/24–8/30/4/1–3/22–3/13–7/2/52/49–51/3–4/61/59–60/2–4/6–9/72–3/70/4/1/5/9/8	Brush B32F	1925
Nos 519–21/3/569	HA 2455/7/6/8/3503	Brush/BMMO B32F	1924
Nos 538/43/5–7/9/51–6/8/60–4/7	HA 2477/80/7–8/1/3/5/–6/9–90/2/1/4/6–99/3501/4	Ransomes B32F	1925
No. 574	HA 3509	Carlyle B32F	1926
No. 586	HA 3511	Brush B32F	1926

The S types that were in original condition and not rebuilt to SOS ODDs were all taken out of service between 1928 and 1934.

SOS FS Type (Forward Steering)

In 1925, the first forward-control single-deckers were introduced. 572, (HA 2500), was the FS model, with thirty-four seats, built by Carlyle. Mechanically it was the same as the S type, with the four-cylinder side-valve 4.344-litre petrol engine and a four-speed gearbox. In its bus form, with a 15 foot 7½ inch wheelbase, the

FS weighed 4 tons 2 cwt. Although it still only had rear wheel brakes, it did have smaller-diameter tyres, enabling the FS type to be 2 inches lower. For the first time, the driver sat over the fuel tank, which was mounted in the cab. Eighty-five further FS types were built for Midland Red. 576–585, (HA 3534–40/2/1/3), were built with Brush bodies, as were 587–94/6–7/99–606/8–9/11–9/21/24–7/31–4/7–40/43–7, (HA 3544–6/9/7–8/50–4/6/9/63–4/0–1/57/55/8/62/5/71/66–7/94/68/70/69/72–7/9/8/81/80/3/91/82/5–6/4/7–8). Most of these buses were withdrawn in 1935.

SOS Q (Queen)

The SOS Q was developed because of BMMO's desire to increase the seating capacity of their standard single-decker from thirty-four to thirty-seven seats. The wheelbase was extended by a foot to 16 foot 7½ inches. This increase in the wheelbase length enabled the body to be fitted with an extra seventh bay, while the length of the cab was reduced with the front bulkhead being moved forward. The prototype vehicle was basically a long-wheelbase FS but, with the exception of the Q prototype, HA 3532, all the other buses had the engine and radiator offset to the nearside enabling the cab space for the driver to be slightly wider. These were the last SOS buses to only have rear wheel brakes.

The Midland Red examples weighed 4 tons 4½ cwt. The Q was 26 feet 6 inches long, 7 feet 2¾ inches wide and 9 feet 5 inches high. One SOS Q, 671, (HA 3599), was fitted with an early six-cylinder engine. 648, (HA 3532), was the only SOS Q built in 1926 and this prototype was delivered to Midland Red. The following year BMMO had a further 109 Qs out of a total of 200 that were constructed. These were 660/662, (HA 3596–7), with Carlyle B37F bodies, and 661/663–666, (HA 3606–10), with similar Brush B37F bodywork. These were soon followed during the same year by Brush-bodied 668–70/2/75–9/81–5/7–7–00/2–3, (HA 3612/1/3/4/16–9/5/26/20/9/7/1/31/3–5/7/63/8–40/22–3/41/4/51), and 671/3–4/80/6/700, (HA 3599/98/3600–2/5).

Finally, there were 704–712/714–720/723/5–8/31/736–779, (HA 3624/43/5/6/25/47/64/48/28/30/2/50/2/65/60/2/61/42/9/59/8/3/54–5/7/6/81/0/91/83/2/4/7/5–6/92/88/93/89–90/3700/7/1–6/8–14/6/5/3697/6/8/5/9/3717–8), all built in 1927 with Brush B37F bodywork, while 729/778–9, (HA 3603–4/94), had Carlyle B37F bodies with the last one entering service in 1928.

The SOS Qs were all taken out of service between 1935 and 1936.

SOS QL (Queen Low)

The SOS QL was a further evolution of the forward-control SOS chassis. It was mechanically the same as the Q chassis of 1927, but they were the first chassis to come out of Carlyle Road Works fitted with four-wheel brakes. The bus was just a quarter of an inch shorter, at 26 feet 5¾ inches, but with the introduction of twin rear wheels, the overall height went down by 2 inches to 9 feet 3 inches. The multi-windowed lightweight body still retained the eight-bay construction of the previous SOS Q and even with the wooden saloon seats weighed just 4 tons 8 cwt 1 qtr.

The QL was only in production during 1928 and were the last of the first generation of BMMO forward-control single-deckers. It was BMMO's most successful model, with many of the buses for Midland Red lasting until 1938. Already withdrawn, the QLs were of little capital value to Midland Red and forty-two QLs were targeted by the War Department – the last one returning to Midland Red in 1943. Additionally, eight QLs were handed over to RAF Shawbury in October 1940, of which four were returned in March 1943 and were in such a poor state that they were immediately broken up. 857, 878 and 886 were used as ambulances from 1940 until the latter part of the war. The last example to be withdrawn was 862, (HA 3781), which survived until 1950.

In all, BMMO built a record total of 381 vehicles in 1928, of which Midland Red took 170 QLs, while another 179 were sold to six other operators.

SOS ODD

By the end of the 1920s, there was a rapidly developing need for a small bus that was suitable for less busy and/or rural services. The result was the SOS ODD type, which was rebuilt and modernised from the SOS S type. Fifty-one of the 1924 chassis were rebodied for Midland Red's own fleet between 1929 and 1930 by United. They had attractive normal-control B26F bodywork mounted on pneumatic tyres, which were 6½ inches wider and, at 9 feet 2½ inches high, were 4½ inches lower than the original S type. The prototype rebuild was HA 2393 and as a result of its success another fifty of these attractive buses were produced, with Trent Motor Traction, Llandudno Blue and Ortona taking 21, 6 and 5 respectively. In their new guise, they proved to be most useful small buses. They were all taken out of service in 1938, though a few were retained as service vehicles.

HA 2327

In order to ascertain the prospect of operating lightweight buses, BMMO purchased fourteen US-manufactured Garford 20 hp chassis. Of these, only five were bodied as buses at Carlyle Works – one of which had a B24F layout while the other four, like HA 2327, had B20F bodywork. They only stayed in service for about three years, but in that time proved that the theory of a fast and lightweight single-decker was viable. HA 2327 stands in front of the main entrance of Carlyle Road Central Works in July 1922 and is labelled for publicity purposes as the 'BMMO CREATION'. (BMMO)

HA 2345

Parked at the Brush bodywork factory in Loughborough prior to delivery in 1923 is HA 2345. This SOS S type was constructed using a Tilling-Stevens TS3 chassis frame and is fitted with Tilling-Stevens radiator header-tank lettering. It was one of fifteen such buses that entered service in 1923 and had a B32F seating capacity. The bodywork on these normal-control single-deckers was typical of the period for such a high-built chassis, with angled rocker panels, a six-bay construction and a steep, three-step entrance into the saloon. (Brush)

HA 2397

HA 2397 is parked in Hagley Road West at Lightwood Park. This was the nearest point to Bearwood Garage, where the headquarters of the BMMO Company was located. This Carlyle-bodied thirty-two seat SOS S is standing alongside the park railings and is operating on an inbound service to Birmingham. Squeezing past it is a Birmingham Corporation AEC 504, which is working from Quinton to Colmore Row in the city centre. Facing towards Quinton and the fearsome descent of Mucklow Hill is HA 2369, another early Brush-bodied SOS S chassis based on Tilling-Stevens parts. (BCR Library)

HA 2431

The driver and conductor pass the time of day as they wait for their bus, HA 2431, an SOS S with a Brush B32F body delivered in May 1925, to load up with more passengers. The vehicle is standing in Hereford's city centre at the end of High Street in its original condition about two years before it was rebodied as an SOS ODD in 1930. These normal-control single-deckers had a surprisingly high seating capacity, with seats for thirty-one passengers. In its rebuilt format, HA 2431 lasted until 1938. (C. Carter)

HA 2494

Speeding down the main street of Ashby-de-la-Zouch in 1933 is HA 2494, an unrebuilt SOS S with a Ransomes B32F layout dating from October 1925. This bus was not converted to an ODD and was withdrawn in 1934. These buses were instrumental in developing services for the Midland Red Company and were to be found on both urban and long-distance routes. Parked beyond the large Austin Sixteen fabric saloon is HA 2494, another Ransomes-bodied SOS S with a B31F layout also dating from October 1925. On the right is an almost new (late 1932), Leicestershire CC-registered six-cylinder Rover Pilot, noted for its refined specification but gutless performance. (S. L. Smith)

HA 2420

The SOS S class were introduced between 1923 and 1925, but their original high-floored bodies and normal-control layouts were obsolete within four years and so, in 1929, forty-nine of the chassis were selected for rebuilding and were fitted with new United B26F bodies in 1930 and were rebuilt as SOS ODDs. HA 2420 has just arrived on the number 144 service from Worcester and Bromsgrove and is carrying a slip board displaying 'BIRMINGHAM VIA MARLBROOK AND RUBERY'. The bus is standing in Navigation Street alongside the Queen's Hotel with Stephenson Street beyond the SOS M type forward-control single-decker. Most of the ODDs were withdrawn from passenger duties by 1938. (D. R. Harvey Collection)

HA 2433

HA 2433, originally built in 1925 with the BMMO chassis number 99 and fitted with a Brush B32F body, waits outside St Peter's Collegiate Church in St Peter's Square in Hereford city centre. The church was founded in 1035, was rebuilt 300 years later and was restored by the Victorians. HA 2433 was an SOS ODD with an attractive-looking United B26F body that was rebuilt from a Brush-bodied SOS S in 1930. The bus is working on the Weobley via Credenhill service. (D. R. Harvey Collection)

HA 3538

Parked in Pool Meadow bus station is SOS FS HA 3538, with a Brush B34F body dating from 1926. By this time, late in its career, the bus had been converted to four-wheel brakes, which is identifiable by not being able to see through the spokes of the front wheels. Originally, the fuel filler cap was inside the cab, but after a few years the filler cap was fitted externally to just behind the cab door, although the petrol tank was still located beneath the driver's seat. These buses were fleet of foot and quick off the mark and when placed in competition with the Edwardian tram systems of the late 1920s, literally drove the trams off the road. (R. Wilson)

HA 3567

Turning from New Street into Corporation Street in the centre of Birmingham is SOS FS HA 3567, at a time when this main shopping street still had two-way traffic. In the distance is a Corporation AEC 504 with an open-staircase top-covered body. The Midland Red Brush B34F-bodied single-decker entered service in June 1926. The car turning into Stephenson Place behind the white-coated policeman is a small Austin Seven Chummy two-door tourer. In the distance and facing New Street in Victoria Square is the Corinthian-columned Town Hall, which was opened in 1834 and built in the nineteenth-century revival style of Roman architecture, being based on the proportions of the Temple of Castor and Pollux in the Roman Forum. (Commercial Postcard)

HA 3608

In Leicester, at the edge of the Newarke bus station, is SOS Q HA 3608, which was built in 1927. This Carlyle B37F-bodied single-decker is about to work on the 644 service to Countesthorpe by way of South Wigston. Its conductor poses with a passenger and is carrying a Bell Punch ticket machine and a leather money satchel. The SOS Q was basically a long-wheelbase FS, which enabled the seating capacity to be increased by three. For the first time, these buses had the engine set on the nearside. The radiator was also offset to the nearside – a feature that was to become standard on all subsequent pre-war SOS models. This allowed the cab to be slightly more spacious, but the driver still had to sit above the petrol tank in the cab, which had to be filled through the filler cap in the cab! (D. R. Harvey Collection)

HA 3600

In August 1933, HA 3600 is parked in Grantham bus station. This Carlyle B37F-bodied SOS Q bus, built in 1927, has arrived on the long service from Leicester via Melton Mowbray. The bus would be withdrawn in 1936 which, given the lightweight construction of the body, was quite a good innings. The Q was the last model to be built with only rear-wheel brakes and still retained single rear tyres. Parked alongside it is an almost-new Leyland Cub, which is on a service to Melton Mowbray. (G. H. F. Atkins)

HA 3636

Standing on the steep hill in the Bull Ring alongside St Martin's Parish Church in Birmingham is HA 3636. Beautifully painted in a line-out red livery with a white roof, the bus diver looks out of his cab to the rear. He has parked the bus correctly, with the front wheels turned outwards so that if the bus were to roll backwards, it would just run into the kerb. Buses being employed on services using the Coventry, Stratford and Warwick roads had their termini in front of the north door of the mother church of the city, where there was a canteen hut for Midland Red bus crews. The church was rebuilt and redesigned by Birminghan architect J. A. Chatwin, being reconsecrated in 1875. (C. Klapper)

1928–1930: SOS Buses to Extend the System

SOS M (Madam)

The next new BMMO chassis, introduced in 1928, was designed to get more female passengers onto buses. The new model was the SOS M (Madam) and was equipped with more comfortable seating in an attempt to make the vehicles more user-friendly for women. This was the first SOS chassis to have a dropped-frame chassis frame, giving it a lower floor-line, and more luxurious upholstered seats, which resulted in the seating capacity being reduced from thirty-seven to thirty-four.

The first two of the type, 888 and 898, (HA 4907–8), were built with Carlyle bodywork for the Midland Red fleet. After these first two SOS Ms, which had bodies similar to the previous QL model, with straight-sided panels and rocker panels, the rest of the QL buses had deeper, curved lower saloon panels, which gave the SOS M a more modern appearance. In 1929 Midland Red received another forty-seven, but most of the M type production was sold to other SOS operators. 970–1/3–990 and 1022–1044, with non-sequential HA registrations, were built for Midland Red and were mostly bodied by Ransomes, although just one SOS M, 972, (HA 4909), was bodied by Brush. The seven-bay body still retained the raised porch entrance, had radiused windows and a slightly raked windscreen, and for the first time the internal bulkhead partition was omitted. Yet again the weight of the new model was increased to 4 tons 14 cwt, although the wheelbase remained at 16 feet 7½ inches and there were variations according to individual company specifications.

The War Department impressed 888/98/974/90 from 1940 to 1941. The Midland Red Ms nearly all survived the Second World War and were taken out of service between 1947 and 1950.

SOS XL

The XL was the first vehicle designed by the company as a long-distance coach. The chassis incorporated a newly designed six-cylinder 5.986-litre engine and a radiator similar to those used on the later QLC coaches. The Brush and Carlyle-built C30F bodies were modern for a 1929 design, with careful attention paid to a luxurious and well-detailed finish and should, in theory, have been a successful design. Numbered 1045–1087/1089–1095, at the end of 1929 and into 1930 they were all converted to six-cylinder MM (Modified Madam) chassis as they were underpowered and were top-heavy, resulting in poor handling characteristics. All were rebodied in 1930 with new Ransomes B34F bodies, resulting in the early extinction of the model. One of the rebuilt MMs,

1065, (HA 4972), was further rebuilt with a Short B38F ON-style body and ran as such from 1934 until 1937, when the body was fitted to the trial Dennis 'Lancet' DHA 200.

SOS MM (Modified Madam)

During 1929 and 1930 a remarkable number of new types appeared – the situation being further complicated by the extensive reconstruction of some of them after just a few months. In addition to the M model, it was intended that the 1929 production should consist of fifty XL coaches, one prototype COD six-cylinder bus, fifty MM four-cylinder buses and one prototype IM four-cylinder bus. At the heart of these rebuildings, reconstructions and rebodyings were the new SOS MM six-cylinder single-deck buses.

The MM four-cylinder buses with 4.344-litre petrol engines were basically a modification of the M – the only difference being that Ransomes-built bodywork had modified rear-end styling. They were delivered from September 1929 to February 1930 and were numbered 1096–1115 before being converted to IM4 specification with new Short B34F bodies in 1930. Another eighteen four-cylinder MMs were built but their intended Ransomes bodies were fitted to the unfortunate XL chassis, being numbered 1045–1087/89–95, and were converted to six-cylinder MM specification during 1930 with new Ransomes B34F bodies. No more MM four-cylinder chassis were built and the model was replaced by either new or rebuilt IM4s, as 1117–1134, with new Short B34F bodywork.

Of the MM four-cylinder buses, eleven went to the War Department in 1940 and nine were returned within the next two years. All were withdrawn between 1946 and 1950. In 1930, ten six-cylinder MMs with SOS 5.986-litre engines numbered 1136–1145, again with Ransomes B34F bodies, were built and lasted until 1950, when the last seven were replaced by new underfloor BMMO S9 single-deckers.

SOS RR/BRR

Early in 1930, the extensive rebuilding programme began. The bodies of the fifty XL coaches were fitted to new chassis and were designated RR. This was powered by an entirely new six-cylinder engine and had a new type of distinctive flat-topped radiator, which became the BMMO standard design for the next eight years. A prototype bus version of the same chassis was also built, which was designated BRR and became 1246, (HA 5123). It had a new Carlyle-built DP34F body with an angular and sharply raked windscreen. Unusually, the nearside cycle-type mudguard swivelled with the steering.

Another twenty BRRs were built in 1934 as 1479–1498, (HA 9376–9395). These introduced a new 5.580-litre engine and had Short B34F bodies with very deep roofs and radiused saloon windows. They weighed 4 tons 17¾ cwt.

SOS COD

This was also based on the ill-fated dual-purpose XL chassis, but was fitted with a bus body. The body had only five bays and was without the porch entrance. The nominal designer of the bus was Mr P. G. Stone-Clarke, who was Chief Engineer of Trent Motor Traction. There were sixty-one SOS CODs built, of which all but one were the four-cylinder petrol-engined model.

BMMO received twenty-two CODs in 1930 but, like the XL model before it, the Midland Red examples were rebuilt as the new IM4 type and were given new bodies built by Short Brothers. This eliminated the COD as a type operated by Midland Red in just over a year. The single missing chassis was the COD six-cylinder prototype vehicle registered HA 5007, which entered service in 1930 and was fitted by Carlyle with their own B34F body that was distinguished by the D-shaped rear side windows. The bus was fitted with the six-cylinder 6.373-litre engine and was converted to MM specification in 1931. It served as the prototype for Midland Red's ten Ransomes-bodied buses delivered in February to March 1931, which would, after 1944, be numbered 1136–1145, (HA 5012/5127/5/5073–5/7–9/82). A further twenty SOS COD with Brush-bodied vehicles were numbered 1147–1168, (HA 6153–73, not in sequence), and were rebodied with Short B34F bodies in 1931 when they were rebuilt to SOS IM6s. In this form, nine COD/ IM4 were impressed by the War Department, but only two ever came back. HA 5007 remained in service until 1949, while the rest were withdrawn between 1948 and 1950.

796, HA 3726
The bus crew and the inspector pose alongside the Brush-bodied SOS QL HA 3726. The bus had entered service in April 1928 and is parked in Swadlincote in about 1934. The seven-bay bodywork was 2 inches lower than the previous SOS Qs, with a four-step entrance, reflecting that the overall height was reduced to 9 feet 3 inches. The bus would remain in service until 1938 – the year that most of the QLs were taken out of service. It is about to work on the Burton service some 5 miles to the north-west, by way of Stanton. (P. Yeomans Collection)

857, HA 3778
The back of the Brush B37F bodies fitted to the SOS QLs reveals a surprisingly rounded rear with a neatly curved tumblehome. Mounted horizontally under the floor behind the rear axle is the spare wheel. The crew of the bus sitting inside the saloon might be tempted by the delights of the Queen & Castle, an unusual combination of public house and garage in Kenilworth. HA 3778 entered service in August 1928 and was only scrapped in 1949, when numbered 857. (D. R. Harvey Collection)

862, HA 3781
The last SOS QLs to remain in service was 862, (HA 3781), which survived until 1950. With the dreaded 'Do Not Move' or 'No Water' sticker in the windscreen, the bus had only just been withdrawn. The Brush B37F body on the QL was lower than the previous Q model, though the body was still fitted with a pair of life-rails on each side, below the angular rocker panel. What distinguished the QL was they were the first SOS chassis to be fitted with four-wheel brakes and the first to have twin rear tyres. (D. Tee)

HA 4840

HA 4840 was a Ransomes-bodied SOS QL that was delivered in November 1928, and was one of forty-one bodied by the Ipswich-based company over a period of just over four months. The QL model, despite its somewhat antiquated appearance (that was albeit helped a little by having a smooth-topped rather than the older ribbed radiator), quickly obtained a reputation for both speed and reliability. The saloon had a division about two-thirds along the body, allowing for a rear smokers compartment. The bus is parked alongside the rear of the Odeon Cinema in Hereford bus station on 11 August 1939. (J. Cull)

HA 4890

BMMO introduced the QL type in 1928 and nearly 170 were built between then and 1929. Most of the bodies of this class were built by Brush and seated thirty-seven passengers. These vehicles were among the last to have a rocker-panel style of body and were the first SOS buses to have equal-sized wheels all-round. 922, (HA 4890), given this fleet number in 1944, is in Bearwood during September 1950. It was withdrawn from service three years earlier and is being used as a driver trainer. As a safety precaution for the trainee and the instructor, the fuel tank was removed from beneath the driver's seat! (S. N. J. White)

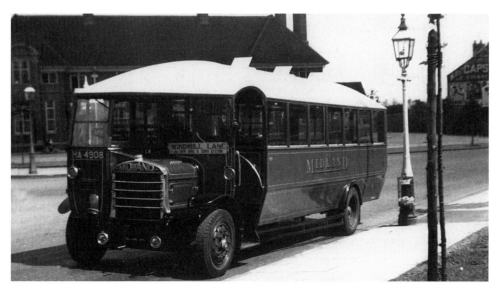

898, HA 4908

In 1938, waiting at the terminus in Oxhill Road opposite the Uplands Hotel, is the prototype SOS M, 898, (HA 4908). This was the second of the pair of prototypes built with Carlyle B37F bodywork in 1929. When compared to the earlier SOS QLs, the appearance of the bodywork was enhanced by the deeper rocker panels. It is working on the 213 service to Bearwood by way of the New Inns in Handsworth and Windmill Lane. (R. T. Coxon)

973, HA 4913

After 1944, the Midland Red bus fleet were given fleet numbers that corresponded to the A series numbers. 973, (HA 4913), is an SOS M with a Ransomes B34F body, which dates from April 1929. These buses had subtly more curved rear panelling and looked distinctly more up-to-date than the previous QL model. It is parked in St Margaret's bus station in about 1947 and would be taken out of service two years later. The comparison between the contemporary Brush and Ransomes bodies was subtle, but distinguishing features were that the small nearside canopy bracket was smaller on the Ransomes-bodied vehicles, whose saloon windows had slightly more radiused tops. (D. R. Harvey Collection)

1024, HA 4937

On 21 August 1949, 1024, (HA 4937), is parked in Spiceal Street with the Bull Ring behind 2537, (GHA 972), a war-time Duple-bodied Daimler CWA6. 1024 was an SOS M, known as a Madam, with a Ransomes B34F body that had entered service in July 1929 and was one of five of the class that survived in service until 1950. To the right is the churchyard of St Martin's Parish Church. Buses usually unloaded and loaded up in the Bull Ring, where the double-decker is parked, but if that narrow area was congested with buses, then they would wait around the corner in Spiceal Street, to load up with a traffic inspector directing passengers to the parked buses. (D. Tee)

1038, HA 4948

The imposing, arcaded Warwick Town Hall was located in the Market Place and was built in 1670. Some of the bus services coming into the county town from the west used New Street as a terminus, and parked alongside the impressive seventeenth-century building. 1038, (HA 4948), a Ransomes B34F-bodied SOS M, stands at this turning point in 1947, two years before it was withdrawn. These buses had slightly raked windscreens and steel external body panels, as well as bucket seating and no internal partition. (A. Porter)

1092, HA 5050

The MM6 single-deckers were all built with a revised, somewhat plain radiator and a new, more substantial style of nearside front wing, thereby modernising the appearance of these buses. 1092, (HA 5050), is parked on Coalville bus station on 8 October 1949 having arrived from Leicester on the 665 service. Originally built in 1929 as an SOS XL, it never ran as such, and was rebuilt into a MM6 chassis with a 5.986-litre six-cylinder engine. The bus received a new Ransomes B34F body, which was among the last built by the Ipswich-based coachbuilder for Midland Red. They had a curvaceous rear with rounded rear windows and an uplift in the rear waist rail. As with most of the MM6s, this bus was withdrawn in 1950. (D. Tee)

1102, HA 5116

Parked in Jamaica Row, Birmingham, in 1947 is 1102, (HA 5116), an SOS IM4 with a Short B34F layout. The IM4s as a group had at least three types of radiator and 1102 carries the earliest style. The IM4 chassis was the last single-decker to use the four-cylinder 4.3-litre petrol engine. Originally built as a MM Modified Madam in 1929, with a Ransomes body, the class of twenty buses were converted to IM4 (Improved Madam) and were rebodied with new Short B34F bodies that were only 9 feet 3 inches high, but were equipped with more comfortable seats. It is waiting to return to its home town of Tamworth and was withdrawn in 1948. (A. Porter)

1153, HA 6158

The 'COD' was based on the underpowered and short-lived XL coach chassis but had a bus body and was originally built to be used on long-distance stage carriage services. The buses were originally built with four-cylinder engines and Brush bodywork, but were equipped in 1931 with new Short Brothers bodywork, becoming IM4s. Shorts had taken over from Ransomes as a supplier of bodywork to Midland Red and immediately produced a more modern-looking product. The number of side windows was reduced to six by increasing the distance between the pillars, which resulted in the lengthening of the saloon window bays, and the old raised porch roof over the entrance steps was eliminated. The majority of the sixty CODs went to Potteries and Trent and remained unrebuilt, whereas the twenty-two that went to Midland Red became IM4s. 1153, (HA 6158), stands in the centre of Ashby-de-la-Zouch with its front wheel chocked with Midland Red's own brass fitting on 8 October 1949. (D. Tee)

1930–1934: Buses Taken Over and Early 1930s SOS Buses

Ex–Great Western Railway

Eight vehicles arrived from the Great Western Railway on 23 May 1930 when their Black Country services were compulsorily taken over. Numbered 1235–1242, they were, with one exception, typical of the standard buses operated by GWR. 1235, (UU 4814), and 1237, (YU 4107), had Maudslay ML3A chassis with Vickers B32F bodies and dated from 1929 and 1927 respectively. While 1236, (YU 4106), and 1238, (RF 3348), were also Maudslay ML3A, but with Birmingham-built Buckingham bodies and dated from 1927, 1239, (YE 7310), was a Guy FBB with a Buckingham B32F body built in 1927, while 1240–1241, (RF 2457/2869), were normal-control Maudslay MLs with B26F bodies by Buckingham. The most modern bus was 1242, (RF 4964), which was an early Leyland Tiger TS1 with a Leyland B30F built by 1928. 1238/40–2 were originally owned by F. E. Weston, trading as Blue Bus, of Four Ways, Cradley Heath, who had been taken over by GWR in April 1929.

SOS IM4 (Improved Madam Four-Cylinder)

The two Improved Madam prototypes with Carlyle B34F bodies entered service in 1929 as 1116, (HA 5085), in the Midland Red fleet and 1245, (HA 6226), which went directly to Potteries. The IM4 model was the last of the SOS chassis to be built with the original 4.344-litre SOS petrol engine and was a development of the SOS MM and the COD type. The body had deep, curved side panels and a straight nearside roof-line, as well as a three-step entrance. The earliest of the buses had the large header tank atop the radiator and were the last SOS buses to have the four decorative horizontal bars on the radiator, which seemed to be a final hurrah to the old Tilling-Stevens buses. The buses were 26 feet 2 inches long and 7 feet 4½ inches wide but were higher at 9 feet 6 inches, and weighed about 4 tons 12 cwt.

The 1933 deliveries, classified as IM4Ds, had a more modern appearance, with radiused saloons with half-drop opening windows, glass side window louvres and no roof overhang above the windscreen. The 1931 vehicles were numbered 1247–1296 and the 1933 IM4s, numbered 1449–1478, had Short B34F bodies. The vehicles built in 1932, delivered between March and June, were 1320–1368 (starting with HA 8247), and had Brush bodies, with the exception of 1344, (HA 8295), which had a metal-framed MCCW B34F body weighing 4 tons 15 ¾ cwt. A total of eighty-nine IM4s were sold to other BET operators.

From the fifty Short Brothers-bodied IM4s, seventeen were impressed by the War Department in 1940 but only four were ever returned to Midland Red. Withdrawals took four years to complete, with the last sixteen going in 1950. The same pattern was repeated with 1449–1478, when eleven were taken by the War Department and just seven were returned by 1942, although 1451, (HA 8351), was in such poor condition that it was broken up immediately after its return. The rest were all withdrawn in 1950 and 1951.

SOS IM6 (Improved Madam Six-Cylinder)

This was the first large-scale production SOS model to have the six-cylinder 5.986-litre SOS RR2SB engine. The SOS IM6 single-decker was produced concurrently with the IM4 chassis. These buses were fitted with a new crash gearbox, which had a 'silent third' gear. The new flat-topped radiator introduced on the IM4s was used but was longer in order to cool the larger engine. Although the first of the BMMO IM6s were fitted with Brush bodies taken from the SOS COD types, those supplied to operators elsewhere were constructed by Short Brothers with a B34F layout, a deep-roofed six-bay body and weighed about 4 tons 17 cwt with a height of 9 feet 3 inches.

Brush B34F, ex-COD-bodied 1297–1318, (HA 6227–6245/7326–7328), entered service in 1931 and 1299–1302/4–5/13–5 were impressed by the War Department in 1940, all of which were returned to Midland Red in 1942. 1297–1301/3/7–10/25 ran on producer gas and operated from Evesham Garage during 1943 and 1944. All of the first batch of IM6s were withdrawn between 1950 and 1952.

The second group were numbered 1420–1447, (HA 8296–8323), and arrived in 1933 with Short B34F bodies. Four – 1422/9/32/9 – were impressed by the War Department from 1940 and all except 1429 were returned in 1942 for further service. 1441, (HA 8317), was the prototype conversion to producer gas in 1942 and was followed by the further conversions of 1420–3/6–8/30–1/3/6/8/40/42–44 to producer gas in 1943, which were used by Evesham Garage. Reverting to petrol power in 1944, all were eventually withdrawn between 1950 and 1952.

YU 4107

Former Maudslay ML3A YU 4107 was previously owned by the Great Western Railway as their 1530. First entering service on 30 November 1927 with Blue Bus of Cradley, it passed to GWR on 2 April 1929. The railway services in the Black Country were taken over on 23 May 1930 by Midland Red. During its brief sojourn with Midland Red, YU 4107 was transferred to Hereford along with RF 2869, a 1927 normal-control Maudslay ML3 with a Buckingham B26F body, which is parked behind it. Both of these former Blue Bus vehicles, by then painted in Midland Red livery, were sold to Western National in May 1930. Both buses are outside St Peter's Collegiate Church in St Peter's Square in Hereford city centre. (D. R. Harvey Collection)

RF 2869

Having been taken over from Weston's Blue Bus Service of Cradley Heath by the Great Western Railway in August 1929, RF 2869 was quickly repainted into GWR's bus livery. Weston's operated their small bus fleet on routes to Dudley, Netherton and Old Hill. The GWR services ran for the last time on 23 May 1930. RF 2869 was a 1927-vintage Maudslay ML3 and had a Birmingham-built Buckingham B26F body. It was eventually sold to Western National, becoming their 3053. (D. R. Harvey Collection)

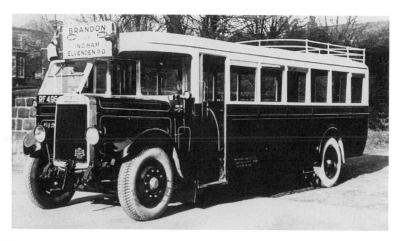

RF 4964

The newest of the original Weston fleet was a very early 1928 Leyland Tiger TS1 fitted with a Leyland B30F body. After being acquired from the Great Western Railway in May 1930, the bus was quickly sold to the West Yorkshire Road Car Company, where it became their fleet number 519. By this time, it had received a later style of radiator. The Leyland body was eventually converted into a parcels lorry. (F. W. York)

HA 6201

In about 1935, Midland Red SOS IM4, an Improved Madam single-decker with a four–cylinder petrol engine, and a thirty-four-seat Short Brothers body dating from 1931, stands outside John Devoti's confectionery shop just beyond the Hurst Street junction, in Smallbrook Street. It is loading passengers for the 147 service to Alvechurch and Redditch. Despite their antiquated looks, these lightweight buses were considered to be very fast for their time, being the equal, in performance terms, with the products of the major proprietary manufacturers. HA 6201 would be numbered 1279 in 1944 and would survive in service until 1950. Behind the bus is the entrance to the Empire Theatre, which was destroyed in an air raid on 24 October 1940. Smallbrook Street's buildings, including that of George Hull (a dry salter, oil, varnish and paint manufacturer), on the far corner of Hurst Street, would disappear in the redevelopment of the area in the early 1960s. (Warwickshire Local Studies)

HA 6228

Even with the privations of wartime, Midland Red still managed to provide bus services to the more remote parts of the operating area. On Thursday, 5 September 1940, HA 6228, a 1931 six-cylinder, Brush B34F-bodied SOS IM6, is parked next to the RAC shed at British Camp in the Malvern Hills (an Iron Age hill fort located at the top of Herefordshire Beacon, dating from the second century BC). This was at the end of the Battle of Britain and virtually marked the end of Luftwaffe attacks on RAF airfields, but here in Herefordshire the war could have been a million miles away, with the only evidence for it being the blackout paint and masked headlights on this bus. HA 6228 was later briefly fitted with a producer gas trailer when based at Evesham Garage. (J. Cull)

1311, HA 6241

1311, (HA 6241), was one of twenty SOS IM6s that were delivered in 1931. It was fitted with a 1930 Brush B34F body that had been formerly fitted to an SOS COD, which is distinguishable by the greater clearance of the lower side panels. These Brush-bodied buses weighed just over 5 tons and had a poorer power-to-weight ratio when compared to the lighter Short-bodied examples. On 12 August 1950, HA 6241 is seeing out its final days of service in Shrewsbury while working on the S1 town service to Ragleth Gardens. The IM6s with the six-cylinder 5.986-litre petrol engine had a new, deeper style of flat-topped radiator. (D. Tee)

1441, HA 8317

HA 8317 was the first of seventeen SOS IM6s from the 1933 batch to be converted to producer gas operation. This bus entered service with this equipment in 1942 after the Ministry of War Transport gave instructions that, in order to save on valuable petrol, 10 per cent of all bus fleets with over 100 vehicles were to be equipped to operate with producer gas, using a special trailer with a coke stove, gas washers and condensers. Midland Red equipped thirty of its older buses and ran them on a number of routes. Crews were required to rake out the furnace of each trailer and refuel it from the sacks of coke that were carried on the bus. The flow of combustible gas was often insufficient for consistent performance and hills were a nightmare for drivers and passengers. The exhaust gases emitted from the long flue pipe were lethal, with the awful rotten eggs-like smell of hydrogen sulphide. This Short B34F-bodied single-decker ran with this type of trailer until the latter part of 1944. (BMMO)

1461, HA 8356

Opposite above: Parked in the bus station in Swadlincote on 8 October 1949 is Short B34F-bodied SOS IM4 1461, HA 8356. This batch of twenty buses built in 1933 and 1934 were the last IM4s to be constructed and were also the last SOS buses to have the SOS four-cylinder 4.3-litre petrol engine. The last twenty of the class were reclassified IM4D (Improved Madam Development), and with their Short B34F bodies had an increased unladen weight of 4 tons 14 cwt. The Short bodies had a deep, rounded roof contour, no projection over the windscreen and a prominent support bracket on the nearside of the canopy. The six half-drop side windows had radiused corners and the deeper side panels continued the gradual modernisation in the development of the Midland Red body style. The whole effect was somewhat spoilt by the motorcycle-styled single-radius nearside mudguard. (D. Tee)

1481, HA 9378

The solitary SOS BRR of 1930, HA 5123, looked nothing like the twenty BRRs built in 1934. These had Short B34F bodies that were similar to the final batch of IM4s. They had the new SOS six-cylinder 5.580-litre petrol engines coupled to the latest silent third gearbox. 1481, (HA 9378), is swimming its way into Ironbridge in 1947 alongside the flooded River Severn, whose breached bank is just beyond the iron railings. It is not easy to see if the conductor is about to measure the depth of the water with his foot, hurdle onto the bonnet top, or just abandon ship and go for a swim! (D. R. Harvey Collection)

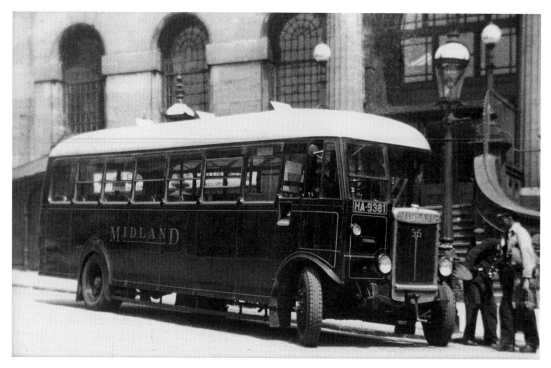

HA 9381

Parked in Worcester Street on Monday, 3 July 1939 is HA 9381. This SOS six-cylinder BRR has a Short B34F body and stands in front of the rear entrance to the Market Hall. Designed by Charles Edge, the architect of Birmingham Town Hall, the Market Hall opened on 12 February 1835 and contained 600 market stalls. The building was faced with stone from Bath, its impressive wide entrances were supported by Doric columns and the building was 365 feet long, 180 feet wide and 60 feet tall. Just over a year later, on 25 August 1940, the Market Hall was severely damaged by an incendiary attack in one of the first heavy air raids of the war. HA 9381 would be numbered 1484 in 1944 and would remain in service until 1951. (J. Cull)

1934–1937: Later SOS Single-Deckers

By 1934, a new, second generation of BMMO half-cab single-decker buses was introduced, being classified as the SON type. With their six-cylinder, compact, short-length petrol engines, silent third gearbox, longer wheelbase and the body length being increased to 27 feet 6 inches, the SOS ONs had a seating capacity of thirty-eight and were the forerunner of some 583 buses based on the new chassis.

In 1934 the DON type was introduced using the AEC 7.58-litre oil engine, while from 1935 onwards Midland Red developed its own K type 8.028-litre oil engine, which was noted for its smooth running performance. ON types were converted in 1936 and classified as CONs (Converted ON).

Until 1935, the SOS chassis were distinctly odd-looking, though the reasons for their peculiarities were quite logical. The SOS petrol engines, fitted along the central line of the chassis, were very short-length units, which enabled the front bulkhead to be placed close to the rear of the front axle. The Midland Red vehicles, however, retained a somewhat idiosyncratic appearance, with narrow cabs, offset radiators and the fuel tank being located in the cab beneath the driver's seat! Yet, because of these design features, in the late 1930s the SOS SON single-decker had a seating capacity of thirty-eight with a weight of about 5½ tons, which was around the same as the SOS buses being built at the beginning of the decade and about four more than bodies built on more convertional chassis.

SOS ON (Onward)

Midland Red introduced its new SOS ON model in 1934. A total of 131 of the petrol-engined SOS ONs were built between 1934 and 1936 and of these Midland Red received eighty-three. These were the last of the SOS design to be supplied to more than one other member of the BET Group. The ONs were built to the new maximum length of 27 feet 6 inches for two-axle single-deck buses and coaches. This, coupled with the compact SOS RR2 LB 6.373-litre petrol engine and silent third gearbox, enabled the bonnet length to be very short, which in turn allowed a longer space for the passengers, enabling the capacity to be increased to thirty-eight seats. The bodies built by Short Brothers were 27 feet 5¾ inches long on a wheelbase of 17 feet 6⅜ inches. The new design of the Short bodywork was more subtly curved and modern, with a moulded waist rail and large, radiused corners to both the half-drop saloon windows and the windscreen.

There were two series of these petrol-engined ONs, which were numbered 1500–1535, (HA 9451–86), and 1592–1641, (AHA 487–536). Two ON buses were equipped with engines built by other manufacturers, with 1506 having a Dorman four-cylinder oil engine and 1533 having a Leyland 8.6-litre oil engine. Within four years, all but the last one of the first batch were converted to CONs, as well as twelve of the second group, totalling forty-four vehicles. All were fitted with the new BMMO 8.028-litre diesel engine developed in 1935.

During 1940, twenty-seven CONs were converted to ambulances. The privations of war resulted in seventeen bodies being unflatteringly rebuilt by Carlyle between 1947 and 1949 with new all-metal sides and un-radiused windows, almost to a utility design. The twenty-six bodies were rebuilt by Nudd Brothers at the same time as their contract for Brush-bodied SOS FEDD double-deckers. A further nine were rebuilt by Hooton in 1952 and lost their decorative waist mouldings with rubber-mounted windows. Withdrawal of the ON/CON buses took place between 1950 and 1957.

SOS LRR (Low Rolls-Royce)

In 1932, Midland introduced a new thirty-seat coach. This was the LRR type and was based on the REDD type chassis with an underslung worm differential, which immediately reduced the overall height of the vehicles, with the saloon area being several inches lower than the narrow, tapered cab. The wheelbase was 17 feet 6 inches long and was, when fitted with an attractive, if somewhat quirky Short Brothers body, 27 feet 4½ inches long. The coaches weighed 5 tons 16 cwt 1 qtr. These coaches had the newly introduced SOS RR2 LB 6.373-litre petrol engine, which was coupled to a five-speed crash gearbox. 1586–1590, (HA 9396–9400), of 1934 and 1642–1666, (AHA 587–611), of 1935 were all converted to B34F-layout buses in 1940 and 1941 as they were surplus to requirements as coaches, and survived until 1952.

SOS OLR (Open Low Rolls-Royce)

All twenty-five SOS OLR normal-control touring coaches were built for Midland Red in 1935 in order to replace the SOS QLCs, which had entered service between 1928 and 1930. The OLR chassis was a new design with a 17 foot 6 inch wheelbase, swept frames similar to FEDD-style chassis frames and axles with underslung worm drive on the rear. The engine was the 6.373-litre RR2LB powerful petrol unit, which was coupled to a modified silent third gearbox.

A new type of radiator was fitted that was unique to the OLRs and similar to the 1930 QLC 6 inch types. The Short Brothers twenty-nine-seat bodies had roll-back canvas roof covers and sliding front entrance doors. 1667–1691, (AHA 621/612–620/622–636), were the last open coaches and the last normal-control chassis produced by the company.

The OLRs were used as buses during the early part of the Second World War but, like the LRRs, were converted to buses in 1941 and 1942 immediately after the

LRR rebuilds. The chassis were rebuilt to forward-control and a permanent saloon roof was fitted to a body with a B34F seating layout. They remained in service until 1952.

1518, HA 9469

Above: Standing in the parking area in Stourbridge bus station, in front of Stourbridge Town railway station, is 1518, HA 9469. This was a 1934-vintage SOS ON with a Short B38F body. It was converted from a petrol engine to a CON with a BMMO 8.028-litre oil engine in 1937. 1518 was rebuilt by Nudd Brothers & Lockyer of Kegworth in 1950 with rubber-mounted saloon windows with sliding ventilators and survived until 1956. (A. D. Broughall)

1529, HA 9480

Overleaf above: Operating on a Shrewsbury town service is HA 9480, a 1934 Short-bodied SOS ON. This was converted in 1938 to a CON with a SOS 8.028-litre oil engine while it was rebuilt by Nudd in 1949 with rubber-mounted glazing in the saloon. This gave the bus another seven years' service, although it did look rather severe after it was reconstructed; only the windows around the cab area remained unaltered. (M. Rooum)

1595, AHA 490
Stood in Gloucester is 1595, (AHA 490), which is about to return to Worcester on the X72 express service via Cheltenham Spa and Tewkesbury. This SOS ON had been one of the forty-four converted in 1938 to CON (Converted ON) specification by being equipped with a BMMO 8.028-litre oil engine. The Short B38F body had been rebuilt by Carlyle with almost utility-style window panes immediately after the Second World War. (M. Rooum)

1602, AHA 497

The town of Sutton Coldfield had a number of town services, one of which was the S67. This ran a shuttle service between Six Ways, Erdington, to the Parson & Clerk on Chester Road North, Streetly, via the Beggar's Bush in New Oscott. Note just how many public houses were named for timing points! Converted to a CON in 1938 and with its Short bodywork rebuilt in a rather severe style by Carlyle Works, 1602, (AHA 497), is parked in Erdington in the early 1950s in front of a 1934 Ford V8. (A. D. Broughall)

1499, HA 9051

Turning across the Market Square in Warwick in about 1949 is the prototype SOS LRR HA 9051, numbered 1499 and later rebuilt as a thirty-four-seater bus. This was the prototype LRR and when new was the only one of the type to have a five-speed gearbox. The passenger saloon on these coach bodies built by Short was much lower than the driver's cab, resulting in the driving area looking somewhat perched at the front of the vehicle. The heavy sliding door became something of a problem and its location in the second bay was a remnant of its coaching days. (D. R. Harvey Collection)

1656, AHA 601

The SOS LRRs were built in 1935 with Short C30F bodies, but after 1941 they were all demoted from coach work and rebuilt to B34F. 1656, (AHA 601), is parked out of service in Bearwood and has by now been given a fleet number. The lower level of the saloon, reflecting the use of a double-decker back axle and transmission, contrasted with the rather high-mounted driver's cab. Stripped of their luxurious fittings, they were a useful addition to the hard-pressed wartime bus fleet. (A. Porter)

BHA 1

In almost original condition, BHA 1 is posed in 1936. The revolutionary SOS REC had a rear engine and a front entrance alongside the driver. Chief Engineer L. G. Wyndham Shire designed four rear-engined single-deckers in the 1935–6 period, of which BHA 1 was the first. Although very advanced, they were not altogether successful. Shire's successor, Donald Sinclair, used the design concepts of underfloor engines he had pioneered with Northern General when rebuilding all four. (BMMO)

1591, BHA 1

The driver, on all fours, examines the front nearside of the much-rebuilt 1591, (BHA 1), near the entrance to Perry Barr railway station in Birchfield Road. Now classified S1, it is working on the 119 service into Birmingham from the Scott Arms at Great Barr. 1591, (BHA 1), was the first of the RECs to be rebuilt in 1941 with a K type underfloor oil engine and a German ZF 'Aphon' gearbox. This very advanced vehicle was a most curious mixture of 1930s body styles, reminiscent of NGT SE4 types and London Transport's AEC Q's, which combines to produce an extremely strange-looking bus with a raked back front. It was later rebuilt with something akin to a complete S13 front end and a tall, thin, horizontal radiator grill. (R. T. Coxon)

1673, AHA 617

Leaving Hereford bus station, 1673, (AHA 617), is being used on the 425 route to Marden. This was built as an SOS OLR normal-control touring coach. It originally had a retractable canvas roof but with the advent of the war the vehicles were converted to forward control and the body was rebuilt with a fixed roof and a new rear end. The OLRs had a modified double-deck chassis and an underslung differential, allowing for a much lower body line. They had a 6.373-litre petrol engine and a very attractively modern radiator. This OLR was converted to forward control in 1941, becoming a B34F bus. (S. N. J. White)

1685, AHA 630

A rather dusty-looking SOS OLR conversion, 1685, (AHA 630), has just arrived in Shrewsbury bus station on the S9 service from Ditherington in about 1948. From the offside, the difference in height between the driving position and the saloon can be appreciated, reflecting its origins as a touring coach. Parked behind the OLR single-decker is a Reliant 6 cwt three-wheel delivery van with a motorcycle-derived front wheel and headlight. (R. Blencowe Collection)

More SOS Half-Cabs and
Leicester Green

Leicester & District, Leicester (Leicester Green)

In the 1920s and 1930s, there were several different firms running buses to the northwest of Leicester. Leicester & District Green Bus Company was one such operator. Owned by Mr F. H. Gerard of Parr's Garage, based at 88 Church Gate in Leicester, the company was taken over by BMMO on 1 November 1936 on routes from Leicester to Gilroes, Hinckley, Bradgate and Quorn. The fleet at the time of the takeover comprised twenty-three Albion single-deckers dating from between 1924 and 1933, though only six buses were ever actually operated. The fleet were allocated fleet numbers 1945–1967.

Dennis Lancet 2

The chassis of Midland Red's solitary Dennis Lancet 2 was delivered on 26 March 1937 and was initially retained by the Engineering Department for testing. The Short B38F body from the one-off SOS MON HA 5015 was subsequently fitted and DHA 200 entered service on 22 July 1937. It had a Dennis four-cylinder 'Big 4' oil engine and a five-speed gearbox. Its service career was very short with BMMO, as on 23 December 1937 the chassis was sold to South Wales Transport to be their 125. As a result of its short service career with Midland Red, there are no known photos of the bus in its original condition. DHA 200 was rebodied with a Dennis C32F body identical to those fitted to the ten Dennis Lancet 2s delivered in 1938, and remained in service until 1950.

SOS DON (Diesel Onward)

The petrol engines were barely capable of more than about 7 mpg, whereas the recently developed oil engine was far more economical, giving in excess of over 12 mpg. By the early 1930s, SOS needed to evolve its own more economical diesel engine and early diesel SOS buses, known as the DON model, had AEC 7.57-litre indirect injection units. These were 6 inches longer than the SOS petrol unit and the space that was lost reduced seating capacity to thirty-six. Three of the first series, 1530/33–34, (HA 9481/4/5), were built with this AEC diesel engine and were classified as DONs. These were followed in 1935 by a production batch, 1692–1740, which had AHA 537–75/7–86 registrations and the AEC 7.57-litre engine. The AEC engine was longer than the BMMO RR2SB engine, which posed problems, resulting in the front bulkhead being moved back 6 inches and reducing the seating capacity to thirty-six passengers. The AEC diesel engine increased the unladen weight by 4 cwt and weighed 5 tons 7 cwt 2 qtrs. The DON was otherwise similar to the ON in body style and chassis, although the front side windows were noticeably shorter. 1692–5/7–1701/3 were bodied by Brush while the rest were built by Short Brothers. 1706 was fitted from new with a Gardner 5LW engine. The AEC engines were converted to direct injection in 1936.

The DON bodies, like the CONs, were rebuilt, with 1509 being rebuilt by Saunders in 1946, while seventeen were reconstructed by Carlyle in their most severe-looking style between 1947 and 1949, another twenty DONs were rebuilt by Nudd Brothers and the final twelve were rebuilt by Hooton in 1952. All were withdrawn between 1953 and 1957.

SOS SON (Saloon Onward)

The production SOS SON was a natural development of the ON and DON models. The BMMO SON was fitted with an 8.028-litre direct injection oil engine, which was coupled to a four-speed silent third gearbox. Midland Red's first examples were bodied by English Electric, who, after Shorts ceased building bus bodies, briefly became the company's alternative body supplier. The last two batches for the company received Brush B38F bodies in two distinct styles. A total of 254 SOS SONs were built for Midland Red with only Trent Motor Traction buying a further twenty-six SONs, twelve of which were delivered in 1939 and fourteen in 1940, all with Willowbrook B34F bodies – the latter being the very last SOSs built. The 280 SONs were the last of the half-cab single-decker SOS type to be constructed.

The prototype SON, 1741, (AHA 576), was powered by the RR2SB 5.986-litre petrol engine that was coupled to a rather complex and less-than-reliable Cotal epicyclic gearbox, which used electromagnets, a steering column switch and was two-pedal control. This gearbox was later placed in the REC1 prototype BHA 1. 1741 was fitted with a Short B38F body that had been removed from an ON. When the first production batch of sixty-five SONs appeared in 1936, the petrol-engined AHA 576 was re-classified 'ON'.

The first production SONs were 1877–1941, (CHA 501–565), and were fitted with the 8.028-litre K type oil engines with a standard silent third gearbox and English Electric bodies, whose styling was similar to the previous ON and DON types but with major differences: the emergency door was moved to the off-side, behind the front bulkhead, and the five seats across the rear replaced the old rear emergency door. This increased the capacity to thirty-nine. The main saloon entrance was fitted with a sliding door, which replaced the previous porch arrangement. Half-drop windows were fitted and the rear wheels were covered. Most of this batch was reconstructed, with Nudd Brothers completing thirteen in 1949 and 1950 and Hooton rebuilding another thirty-nine in 1951 and 1952. The rebuilds had rubber-mounted windows with sliding ventilators, which replaced the half-drops. The waist rail mouldings were removed and most buses lost their sliding entrance doors in favour of a porch arrangement. Normal withdrawals began in 1953 and were concluded in 1958, when thirty-two were withdrawn.

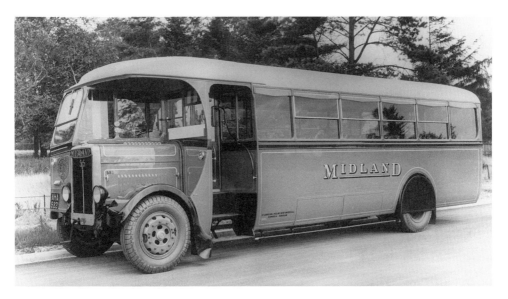

1698, AHA 583
The paintwork on the brand-new SOS DON AHA 583 looks most impressive with its maroon-painted waist rail as it poses at the Brush grounds in Loughborough in 1935. This single-decker sat thirty-six passengers and because of the slightly longer bonnet due to the longer AEC engine, which intruded into the platform area, the body pillars were adjusted, with the first bay being shorter than the remainder. The bus was taken out of service during 1956, having been renovated by Nudd in 1950. (Brush)

1699, AHA 584
Parked in St Margaret's bus station in about 1948 is a SOS DON fitted with a Brush B36F body delivered in August 1935. 1699, (AHA 584), is still in original condition, with a moulded waist rail below the saloon windows. It still has the Midland Red garter on the front cab apron and is fully lined-out. When it was rebuilt in 1950 by Nudd Brothers the body mouldings and the glass louvres were removed. The bus was withdrawn in 1955. (D. R. Harvey Collection)

1732, AHA 567

Loading up with passengers in Burton bus station is 1732, (AHA 567). This SOS DON had a Short B36F body and entered service in 1935. It is working on the 668 service to Leicester by way of Coalville. 1732 was one of the buses renovated by Nudd Brothers in 1949 with rubber-mounted saloon windows and sliding ventilators. Prior to being rebuilt, many of these vehicles had sagging bodywork after receiving little or no maintenance during the Second World War. (R. Marshall)

1880, CHA 504

One of the early English Electric B39F-bodied SOS SONs is in Hereford, working on the H8 route to Putson. 1880, (CHA 504), entered service in 1936 and was one of the earliest withdrawals, being taken out of use in 1953 without ever being rebuilt, retaining the body mouldings with glass louvres above half-drop saloon windows. All is not well with this body, as the half-drop windows are twisted in their frames. (S. N. J. White)

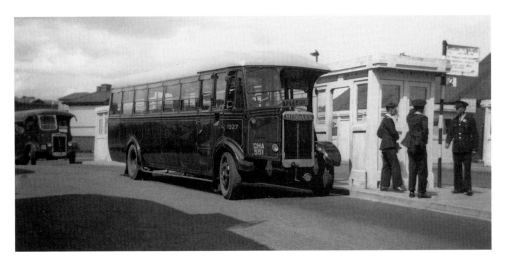

1927, AHA 561

As yet unrebuilt, 1927, (AHA 561), a 1936 SOS SON, is parked in Worcester bus station having worked on the 356 service from Peopleton. The emergency exit was behind the offside of the front bulkhead, giving an untidy multiple-windowed effect, though it did eliminate the centrally located rear emergency exit. The waist rail on the English Electric B39F body does not look straight, especially on offside of the cab area, but it would be 1952 before it would become one of the last bodies to be renovated by Hooton. (A. D. Packer)

RY 4830

Parked outside the Leicester & District bus garage is RY 4830. This Albion PM28 had a Dodson B32F body, which, although lower than the contemporary 1927 Midland Red SOS Qs, the front of the Albion chassis, with its exposed steering column and square radiator set back almost above the front axle, looked positively antiquated. Yet, the Leicester Green fleet of Albions were fast and comfortable and provided sufficient competition in the Leicester area for Midland Red to take them over on 1 November 1936. (Southdown Enthusiasts)

RY 5863

The driver, Christopher Hubbard, and his conductor, William Fowler, stand in front of RY 5863, an Albion PM28 with a neat-looking Northern Counties B32F body. The driver's cab was the most vintage part of these buses, with a steering wheel mounted more like something found on an Atlantic liner! This bus entered service in January 1928 and is working on the Leicester to Quorn route during the following year. The route to Quorn was the main service provided by Leicester & District. (D. R. Harvey Collection)

JF 4874

Only six buses of the twenty-three taken over from Leicester & District on November 1936 were ever operated and all were Albions. Although they were repainted in Midland Red livery, they lasted barely a year before being sold. One of the last to be bought in July 1933 was JF 4874, the first of a pair of Albion PV70s with Duple coach bodies. They were really dual-purpose vehicles, seating thirty-five and had a rear entrance. JF 4874 is parked in Bearwood Garage yard in 1937. (D. R. Harvey Collection)

The Last SOS Half-Cabs, Ex-War Department Returns and Rear-Engine to Underfloor Buses

The second SON production batch of 100 had the first twenty-seven arriving in 1937 and the balance being delivered in 1938. Numbered 2019–2118, (DHA 637–736), the bodies were again built by English Electric, but they reverted to the ON thirty-eight-seating capacity with a traditional porch entrance and rear emergency door. The bodies had shaped pillars that were wider at the top and full-drop rather than half-drop windows. Again, rear mudguards, somewhat impractically, completely covered the tyres in an attempt to produce a streamlined effect. The cab was slightly wider and now projected a few inches over the radiator and bonnet, giving the driver a little more elbow room. The fuel tank was mounted on the offside of the chassis frame, thus allowing a conventionally glazed cab door arrangement. Unlike the other SONs, this particular series was never rebuilt and remained almost original until withdrawal. One vehicle in the batch, 2034, (DHA 652), received a lightweight Carlyle body in 1938. From September 1939 until the latter part of 1940, eight of these buses, 2056/95/8/2101/7/10/2/4, were converted into stretcher-bearing ambulances. Withdrawals took place over a five-year period from 1952 until 1956, when the last seven went.

In 1938, a batch of fifty SON buses appeared, again fitted with English Electric thirty-eight-seat bodies. These were 2169–2218, (EHA 737–786, but not in sequence). This final batch of Preston-built bodies was to a third design, with the fuel tank reverting to beneath the drivers' seat, but the cab side was an improvement on earlier designs. Like the DHA series, this batch was never heavily rebuilt in later life. 2208, (EHA 786), received the prototype lightweight 'Skin and Bone' body built at Carlyle Works, which was originally mounted on the chassis of DHA 652.

Another thirty-eight SONs with Brush B38F bodies began to enter service between May and October 1939, numbered 2294–2331, (FHA 449–86). Thirty-seven of them were basically similar to the EHA batch but were fitted with the newly styled FEDD radiator. They were fitted with German ZF Aphon gearboxes with helical gears on the second and third gears, which produced a virtually silent gearbox. 2313, (FHA 468), carried a lightweight Brush body with a half-canopy and a completely restyled rear end, with the rear bay having a down-turned waist rail. Only one bus, 2310, (FHA 465), was rebuilt at Carlyle Road Works in 1950. All but 2325, which was withdrawn in 1954, were rebuilt by Nudd Brothers between 1950 and 1951 with unflattering rubber-mounted, almost caravan-style windows, sliding saloon ventilators and the removal of the waist mouldings. They were mainly withdrawn between 1957 and 1958.

The last SOSs built for the company's use were fifty attractively Brush-bodied SON thirty-eight-seaters delivered between March and July 1940 as 2382–2431, (GHA 301–50). The bodies were more rounded at the fronts and rears than previous batches and had deeper roof profiles. They were also fitted with German ZF Aphon four-speed gearboxes. These buses had the almost AEC-style radiator, which at last gave these final SONs a thoroughly modern appearance. Thirty-seven of the GHA SONs were rebuilt in 1950 by Nudd Brothers and these buses became the last survivors of the class, all being withdrawn by 1958. The very last SOS SONs, however, were fourteen chassis supplied to Trent Motor Traction, which were bodied by Willowbrook and supplied in early 1940. In 1940 Wyndham Shire retired, but although the half-cab single-deck bus went with him, it was what he began in 1935 that, when modified, placed BMMO at the very cutting edge of post-war single-decker bus development.

Ex–War Department Buses

Between July and August 1940, a total of 120 single-deckers were forcibly impressed by the War Department, of which forty-five buses were never returned to Midland Red. These consisted of forty-two SOS QLs, four Ms, sixty-one IM4s and thirteen IM4s, while another eight SOS QLs were handed over to RAFs 11 Flying Training School Shawbury, Shropshire. The buses handed over to the War Department (WD) were used as troop transports, particularly to send troops to the south coast of England to defend the area in the face of the imminent German invasion after the retreat from Dunkirk in May 1940. While in WD service, they were run into the ground with little or no serious maintenance, so that when returned to the company they were frequently in such a poor state that they never ran again. Thirty-four vehicles were returned from Vehicle Reserve Depot (VRD), Slough, in December 1941, while the following month saw a further forty-one buses coming back to Midland Red from the Vehicle Reserve Depot, Ashchurch, near Tewkesbury. In all, forty-five buses were never returned to Midland Red.

Additionally, forty-four former Trent vehicles were sent back to Midland Red, who allocated them fleet numbers 2447–2451 and 2458–2496. Seven assorted Qs, QLs, Ms, a SRR and an IM6 originally from the Northern General Group, which came via VRD Sheffield in 1943 and was immediately broken up by Midland Red, were given fleet numbers 2523–2529. The first batch, numbered 2447–2451, consisted of three SOS CODs and two IM4s. In December 1941, 2448, a SOS COD, and 2450, an IM4, were returned by VRD Slough, while the remaining three came in January 1942 from VRD Ashchurch. Of these, COD 2449, (CH 8911), was the only one to see further service with BMMO. 2458–2496, consisted of five distinct types of former Trent SOS single-deckers and all were sent by the War Department to VRD Ashchurch in June 1942. 2459–2464 were all SOS CODS with Brush B34F bodies, while 2465–2472 were SOS IM4s with Short bodies. 2473-2486 were the six-cylinder-engined SOS IM6s with Short bodies, while 2487-2498 were Brush-bodied SOS IM4s.

2490–2496 were also IM4s, but had Short bodywork. Of these forty-four ex-Trent buses, seven were taken out of service between 1944 and 1946, while seventeen lasted until withdrawal took place between 1947 and 1950.

The Development of the REC and Conversions to S Type Prototypes

An experimental rear-engined single-decker chassis was built by BMMO to the design of Wyndham Shire and his team at Carlyle Road and was designated the REC (Rear Engine Coach). Despite this type description, this first experimental vehicle was bodied with a forty-seat bus body built at Carlyle Road Works. Given the chassis number 1947, it was registered BHA 1. Before it was bodied, the open chassis was road tested, but was fitted with an SOS constant-mesh gearbox. Once bodied in May 1935, and after being demonstrated to the press, in further trials the petrol engine proved difficult to hear and timing the double-declutch gear changes started to become troublesome. As a result, the Cotal gearbox from AHA 576 – the SOS prototype – was fitted and the problem, at least for the drivers, was solved. Thereafter, the Cotal gearbox was adopted for all of the rear-engined prototypes. In May 1935, BHA 1 initially ran as a forty-two-seater but, in order to save £10 in road tax, it was converted to B40F. Testing continued until February 1936, when it entered revenue-earning service at Bearwood Garage.

The Carlyle body had the framework slightly raked towards the rear of the vehicle, which gave it a sleek, workman-like appearance. This vehicle's body was a two-windscreen, flat-fronted, seven-bay construction unit with five half-drop opening ventilators. It was fitted with a rarely used roller blind front destination box, though a route stencil number box, located at the top of the nearside windscreen, was always employed. The two-step open front platform led to a flat-floored saloon, which ran the length of the bus. The bus was one of the first UK single-deckers to be fitted with a set-back front axle, which allowed for an entrance directly opposite the driver's compartment.

The SOS REC had the RR2SB 5.580-litre petrol engine mounted transversely across the rear of the chassis with two radiators – one on either side of the chassis – each covered with vertically slatted ventilation grills. As revolutionary as the rear-positioned engine was, the fitting of the French-built Cotal epicyclic gearbox, which was a semi-automatic, and the two-pedal control unit operated electromagnetically through a Daimler fluid flywheel, was equally unusual. Despite weighing around 5½ tons, the shortened wheelbase of the single-decker coupled with the weight of the engine behind the rear axle led to the steering of the bus being pleasantly light.

The second REC vehicle was a Rear Engine Coach. The coach was registered CHA 1 in April 1936 and was fitted with a Carlyle-built C32C streamlined body. The coach, with the chassis number 2395, also had a Cotal semi-automatic gearbox but was equipped with the larger 6.373-litre petrol engine.

CHA 2 and CHA 3, with consecutive chassis numbers 2396 and 2397, were outwardly very similar to the prototype BHA 1, with both having Carlyle B40F bodies. The main difference was that these two buses were re-engined before entering service with the smaller RR2SB unit. The three REC buses operated from Bearwood Garage in the last years of the 1930s but after war broke out, as their unique components required replacement, including the unavailable spares for the French Cotal gearboxes, so the reliability of BHA 1, CHA 2 and CHA 3 declined and their periods of garage-bound inactivity gradually increased.

The four RECs were virtually off the road by the time of Donald Sinclair's appointment. Using his experience with the NGT SE4 and SE6 side-engined single-deckers, and despite the privations of the war, he decided that these four chassis could be the basis of a completely new design of single-deck chassis.

Donald Sinclair had very different views on future mechanical layouts of buses from his predecessor; his radical premise was to move the engine to between the wheelbase and within the chassis frame. Subsequent events would place large numbers of the production versions of this new breed in service before other commercial manufacturers had barely reached the prototype stage. All four prototypes were withdrawn and dismantled shortly after Mr Sinclair's appointment and reappeared as heavily modified prototypes for the mid-mounted underfloor engine layout that would be favoured when vehicle production resumed in 1946.

The first of the RECs to be converted to an underfloor-engined single-decker was 1591, (BHA 1). Although effectively a new chassis, the new BHA 1 was recorded as 'rebuilt' and was classified the S1 type. Withdrawn and dismantled from May 1940, it re-entered service during the following year with a horizontal version of the standard BMMO K type 8.028-litre oil engine fitted between the chassis frames, with the cylinder heads facing the offside and the crankcase running along the central line of the chassis. The new chassis received a German Zahnrad Fabrik (ZF) Aphon four-speed manual gearbox, which hopefully came out of the Carlyle Road Works stores rather than directly from Friedrichshafen in Germany, as the company were supplying transmission units for Panzer tanks at the time! Midland Red had first used the ZF gearbox in 1938 in both the SOS FEDD double-deckers and the SON front-engined single-deckers, which were both easy to use and virtually silent in operation. A front-mounted radiator was fitted behind a slotted grill located below the windscreen, which prevented overheating problems.

The completed vehicle hardly won any awards for its beauty! Although it barely looked it, the basic body structure was retained, though it was only readily identifiable by the sloping rear panels, the black-painted, bulbously styled mudguard and the curved waist rail of the rear side windows. The seating capacity of forty was kept but a new roofline that sloped from the front to the back of the bus was installed. A completely new front with raked back windscreens followed the same angle as the sloping front bulkhead and the associated front side windows of the saloon. For the first time there was a roller blind and destination number box, though it was so small and at such an angle as to render it practically useless. There was a sliding door across the bulkhead at the front of the saloon and the driver had his own cab door.

Given the fleet number 1591 in the 1944 fleet numbering scheme, BHA 1 was involved in a fatal accident with a petrol tanker in 1951, wherein the front end was severely damaged. The bus re-entered service in 1952 with a vaguely S13-styled front with a set of folding platform doors and the S1 looked much better for the rebuild. In this form, it also had the standard post-war destination box and a quick glance would have suggested a virtually new bus rather than one that was already sixteen years old. It carried on working from Bearwood Garage, where it was known by the platform staff as *The Killer* and was used mainly on Bearwood and West Bromwich locals until it was taken out of service in 1956.

Because of wartime difficulties in obtaining parts, as well as in simply keeping the fleet running, progress was slow in the conversion of the next of the RECs. In 1942, the troublesome coach 1942, (CHA 1), was withdrawn in May 1940 prior to withdrawal, having been delicensed for a couple of years. The original streamlined coach body was sold to Hardwick's of Bilston and the chassis converted to the same underfloor layout as BHA 1. It was reinstated into service during 1942. Mechanically, the vehicle was fitted with the same type of horizontal engine and gearbox as its predecessor, which meant that the bus lost its semi-automatic gearbox in favour of a spare ZF Aphon gearbox. Nominally, the body from CHA 2 was fitted to CHA 1, but there was very little left of the original except for the slightly rearward-sloping body frame. The seven-bay body had saloon windows mounted in rubber with three sliding ventilators on each side and an open porch front entrance, as well as a sliding door to the saloon on the front bulkhead. The sad-looking front windscreen and the double bank of ventilation grills in front of the radiator ensured that the general styling features of the post-war BMMO S6s were laid down with this bus. This second prototype was given the logical designation S2 and was given the fleet number 1942 to correspond to the date of its reconstruction. CHA 1 was withdrawn in 1957.

After the 1944 fleet numbering system was introduced, the next two REC conversions were, similarly, and somewhat unusually, given fleet numbers corresponding to the year they were rebuilt to S types. 1943, (CHA 2), was the next REC to be converted to an underfloor-mounted engine. Exactly the same procedure occurred with CHA 2 as had happened with the previous conversion the body from CHA 3 was fitted to CHA 2 and this was reconstructed so that it looked just like CHA 1 (*this can be difficult to follow, but hopefully the table on page 66 will be of assistance*). The body did differ slightly in that the door to the saloon was a two-piece folding one rather than the previously used sliding one. The only mechanical difference was that CHA 2 was equipped with a Wilson pre-selector gearbox. The body was rebuilt later in life and was the only one of the prototype wartime S classes to be fitted with the larger post-war standard front destination box. Like CHA 1 before it, CHA2 was retrospectively altered, with the top half of the driver's windscreen being recessed, which reduced the reflection of the saloon lights at night. CHA 2 was designated S3 and reinstated during 1943; it was given the fleet number 1943 and it survived until 1957.

The final rebuilding of the last of the four RECs took place in 1944, after it was taken out of service prior to its rebuilding in May 1940. By this time Midland Red had run out of bodies to rebuild so the chassis of 1944, (CHA 3), which reverted to having a ZF four-speed manual gearbox as per CHA 1, received a genuinely new B40F body that was constructed, somewhat slowly, at Carlyle Road. The body was, like all the rebuilds, a seven-bay construction unit and was fitted with a recessed windscreen from new. The main difference from the other two CHA-registered rebuilds was that the body pillars were vertical, as these components were not from a previous body. The body also had saloon windows, which were set in pans rather than mounted in rubber. This made an enormous difference to the appearance of CHA 3, which was classified as an S4.

The most surprising feature of CHA 1, 2 and 3 in their rebuilt state was just how closely their bodies were to the post-war production S6s, whose delivery began in late 1946. Bearing in mind the strict MoWT's diktat on wartime bus-body production, the fact that the new buses utilised beaten or rolled curved panels, that the seats were upholstered, and that half of the saloon windows had opening ventilators were surprising features. Presumably the company was allowed to construct the wartime single-deckers because they managed to manoeuvre their way around the legislation by contending that the buses were rebuilds, even though they looked like completely new vehicles.

The final prototype single-decker was even more revolutionary. Built in 1946, 2579, (HHA 222), was the solitary S5 type. The vehicle was chassis-less with the by now standard 8.028-litre horizontal engine, a constant-mesh gearbox as well as standard running units that were fitted to a body unit built by Metro-Cammell to Midland Red's requirements. Because some of the wartime restrictions had been lifted, the body structure contained quite an amount of aluminium where structural integrity rather than load-bearing was a priority. The body had seven saloon windows with a noticeably widened body frame at the front bulkhead, next to the entrance. There was a single bulkhead door at the top of the saloon steps and the interior, with its forty seats and overhead luggage racks, was almost indistinguishable from the production S6 buses, deliveries of which began only months later, at the end of 1946. HHA 222 was given the fleet number 2579 from new, but like the other prototypes had its appearance spoilt by a somewhat difficult-to-read destination box. Although the chassis-less S5 concept would eventually be the way forward for Midland Red, it would not be until 1954 that the chassis-less S14 buses were built.

The five prototype underfloor-engined single-deckers, BHA 1, CHA 1, 2, 3 and HHA 222, were tried and tested (beginning in 1941) and, by the time these five buses were in operation by 1946, Midland Red were virtually the first operator in the country who had any experience in running underfloor-engined single-deckers. Consequently, in difficult operational conditions, Midland Red were able to trailblaze what other commercial manufacturers had barely placed on the drawing board.

All the prototype S buses seem to have spent most of their lives in the Birmingham and Black Country areas, operating from Bearwood Garage. However, BHA 1 briefly worked in 1943 at Southgate Street Garage, Leicester, as did CHA 1, before withdrawal during 1956–57.

2028, DHA 646

The driver of 2028, (DHA 646), a 1937 SOS SON with an English Electric B38F body, waits patiently for his single-decker to load up with passengers in the St Peter's Square area outside the Shire Hall in Hereford. This large neo-Classical building was designed by Robert Smirke and opened in 1819. The Greek-style Doric columns of the massive portico are a copy of the Theseion in Athens. The building stands behind a large forecourt hidden by the bus shelters. The bronze statue is of Sir George Cornewall Lewis (1806–1863), a man of letters and a statesman who reached the position of Home Secretary under Lord Palmerston and who had connections with Victorian Hereford. (S. N. J. White)

2078, DHA 696

2078, (DHA 696), stands in Bearwood Road outside the exit to Bearwood Garage. The building behind the bus is the main office building of the Birmingham & Midland Motor Omnibus Company. It is waiting for some more poor unfortunates, some of whom will shortly get their first taste of driving a bus when they get behind the driving wheel of this dual-control bus. Ah, the joys of double-declutching! This 1938 SOS SON with an EEC B38F body was withdrawn in 1952 and was converted to a dual-control trainer, with a full front and an extra set of controls for the instructor alongside the trainee. (P. Tizard)

2103, DHA 721

Parked in a remote part of Pool Meadow bus station, Coventry, is 2103, (DHA 721), on 21 April 1956. This is a SOS SON with an English Electric B38F body. These single-deckers had tapered window pillars and fuel tanks mounted more conventionally on the offside rather than under the driver's seat. 2103 was to be withdrawn later in 1956 and, in common with this 1937 batch of EEC bodies, was not rebuilt. With the addition of some extra external strapping on the pillar over the rear wheel arch, this single-decker remained largely unchanged throughout its nineteen-year service life, even retaining the moulded waist rails. (B. W. Ware)

2113, DHA 731

DHA 731 was new to BMMO in April 1938. It was an SOS SON with English Electric B38F bodywork and, after 1944, it was renumbered 2113. It was withdrawn in 1955 and was converted to a tree-lopper by Midland Red before being painted in Stratford Blue's blue and white livery. It was numbered TC1 and was a familiar sight in and around Stratford or at Kineton Garage until December 1963. (D. R. Harvey Collection)

2117, DHA 735

When new, the English Electric-bodied SOS SONs were painted in the style of the SLR coaches, with tapering brown flashes along each side. Coupled with silver trim around the saloon windows and fully lined-out, these buses looked remarkably smart. 2117, (DHA 735), is parked in the Bull Ring in front of St Martin's Parish Church in 1938. Notably, these single-deckers had their fuel tanks mounted conventionally alongside the offside chassis frame and, therefore, the lack of a fuel filler cap in the cab enabled for a much neater cab window arrangement. (R. Wilson)

2182, EHA 750

The body contract for the EHA-registered batch of fifty SOS SONs was again awarded to English Electric, which became the final BMMO buses to have bodies built by the Preston-based coachbuilder. 2182, (EHA 750), is standing outside the Midland Red enquiry office in Wellington when about to work to Much Wenlock and Wrockwardine on the 894 service. Never receiving a body rebuild – suggesting that the quality of the English Electric bodies were well constructed – 2182 was withdrawn in 1954, although the offside centre glass rainshield is missing. (M. Rooum)

2195, EHA 763

On a very wet day, the driver of 2195, (EHA 763), shelters in the porch from the heavy rain. The bus is EHA 763 – an SOS SON with the last type of single-deck body built for the company by English Electric of Preston. 2195 still retains its, by now somewhat sagging, original waist rail and mouldings. It entered service in 1938 and survived without rebuilding until 1953, suggesting that the English Electric bodies were more substantial than the equivalent Loughborough-built bodies. (D. R. Harvey Collection)

2312, FHA 467

Above: By the time 2312 (FHA 467), had been built, in 1939, many of the idiosyncrasies of the previous SOS designs had been eliminated and the result was a rather attractive single-decker. This batch of SOS SONs had the last square style of Brush B38F body. They had the compact 8.028-litre K type oil engine coupled to a German ZF Aphon, with a virtually silent helical-geared gearbox. These buses also featured the new style of FEDD radiator, which helped to mask the narrow windscreen. 2312 is posed for an official Brush photograph in its lined-out red livery with a maroon-painted waist rail and a silver roof. (Brush)

2305, FHA 460

Opposite below: Passengers queue to board 2305, (GHA 460), one of the penultimate batch of 1939 SONs. The 'new look' Christian Dior-styled dress one of the young women is wearing dates the view to about 1951. The Brush-bodied B38F single-decker had been rebuilt by Nudd Bros & Lockyer in 1950 and in the process lost much of the body's pre-war style and panache. The vehicle is loading in Cleveland Road, Wolverhampton, which is better known as the location of the Corporation's trolleybus depot than for being a major town terminus for Midland Red. (S. N. J. White)

Registration	Chassis No.	Seats	New	Converted	Type	Seats	Withdrawn
BHA 1	1947	B40F	1936	1941	S1	B40F	1956
CHA 1	2395	C32C	1936	1942	S2	B40F Ex-CHA 2	1957
CHA 2	2396	B40F	1936	1943	S3	B40F Ex-CHA 3	1957
CHA 3	2397	B40F	1937	1944	S4	B40F New 1944	1958
HHA 222	2894	------	------	-------	S5 1946	MCCW B40F	1958

2313, FHA 468

Above: In the week of 12–18 July 1951, Judy Garland starred in concert at the Birmingham Hippodrome. This was her last venue on her British tour of that year. The billboard in Navigation Street above the bus confirms the date when 2313, (FHA 468), stood at one of the bus stops while working on the 130 service to Stourbridge. It had a modified body, which had a streamlined rear and lacked a half-cab canopy. This body was removed in 1954 and was replaced by a standard Brush body. (S. N. J. White)

2388, GHA 307

Opposite below: Three of the GHA-registered SOS SONs were put into the Driver Training fleet. 2388, (GHA 307), was withdrawn in 1957 and lasted as a tuition vehicle until 1961. Entering service in March 1940 as one of fifty Brush B38F bodied single-deckers, it had been renovated by Nudd Brothers in 1950 and, although fitted with rubber-mounted windows and sliding ventilators, the rebuilding actually quite suited the rounded bodywork in these buses. 2388 is turning out of Hill Street, with its steep hill, into Paradise Street in Birmingham. The driver has driven through the red traffic light in Hill Street as, presumably, he didn't want to do a hill start! (R. F. Mack)

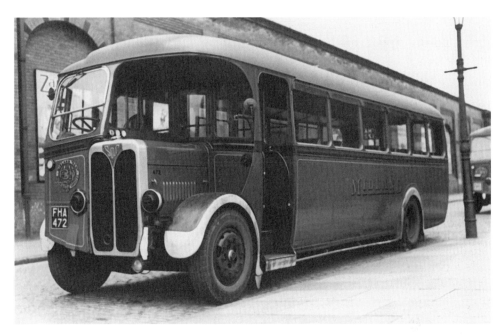

2317, FHA 472
Brush returned to supplying single-deckers on SOS SON chassis and thirty-eight were delivered between May and October 1939. FHA 472 entered service in August 1939 and eleven months later it is parked in Glasshouse Street, Nottingham, in the attractive pre-war livery, with blackout-painted wings and fully masked headlights. These were the first single-deckers to have the new design of radiator, which was introduced on the 1938 EHA-registered FEDDs. The bus has arrived in Nottingham on the long X99 service from Birmingham via Tamworth and Ashby-de-la-Zouch – a journey of just under three hours. (G. H. F. Atkins)

2398, GHA 317

Parked in Hurst Street near Hinckley Street in around 1949 is 2398, (GHA 317). The SOS SON had a Brush B38F body and has yet to be rebuilt by Nudd. These 1940-built buses had a pleasantly rounded rear, a deep roof line and a ribbed waist rail. They had half-drop windows and had the last style of pre-war radiator that had more than a stylistic nod to those on buses built by AEC. By this time, the original SOS logo had been replaced with a new BMMO badge under orders from the new general manager. (R. Marshall)

2470, CH 9925

Former Trent Motor Traction Short-bodied IM4 CH9925 had come back from the War Department in lieu of a genuine Midland Red bus also commandeered by the military. This bus was built in 1931 and it entered BMMO service in 1943, whereupon it was numbered in the Midland Red fleet as their 2470 and lasted until 1947. (J. Cull)

2473, CH 9900

With a metal patch on the side panelling and a sagging cab door, 2473, (CH 9900), looks as though its best days are behind it as it sits in a sunny bus station. This SOS IM6 had a Short B34F body and dated from 1931, when it was delivered to Trent Motor Traction as their 120. Impressed by the War Department in 1940 and numbered M1261760, it was used by them for two years before being returned to Midland Red via the Vehicle Reserve Depot, Ashchurch, near Tewkesbury, when it was renumbered 2473. It was one of the ex-Trent buses that remained in service for the longest period, not being withdrawn until 1950. (D. R. Harvey Collection)

2529, CN 5478

CN 5478, a 1933 Short-bodied IM6, was one of the former Northern General buses that came into the Midland Red fleet in 1943. This is the bus in its original condition when new and is fitted with a huge front destination box, which is a complete contrast to the total lack of such a useful passenger aid on the equivalent Midland Red single-deckers. It came from the War Department storage facility in Sheffield but it never entered service with Midland Red as it was in such a poor state that it was only deemed worthy of being stripped for spares. It was allocated the fleet number 2529. (NGT)

1942, CHA 1

Parked on the forecourt of Stourbridge bus station, in front of the Midland Red Garage facing Foster Street, is the rebuilt 1942, (CHA 1). This was the advanced underfloor-engined BMMO S2 and was formerly the solitary REC coach of 1936. It was reconstructed in 1942 with this advanced Carlyle B40F seven-bay body. The design had all the attributes later associated with the BMMO S6 class, though CHA 1 did have a wider entrance. (D. R. Harvey Collection)

CHA 2

Waiting to load up with passengers in Lower Queen Street, West Bromwich on the 220 service to Bearwood in 1938 is CHA 2. It is barely two years old and shows the large slotted panel on the original body behind the rear axle necessary to improve the airflow to the rear-mounted engine. For all their advanced features, the four RECs were plagued with overheating problems and dust being sucked into the engine. As a result, the buses spent most of their rear-engined lives pottering about the Bearwood area in case they broke down. (R. Wilson)

1943, CHA 2

The rebuilding of CHA 2 in 1943 with a Carlyle B40F body based on the structure removed from CHA 3, produced a seven-bay version of the post-war bodies built on the BMMO S6s. It is parked after working on the 157 route. When first converted to the underfloor-engined S3, the bus had a Wilson pre-selector gearbox. Unlike the body on CHA 1, which had a sliding door across the entrance to the saloon, the rebuilt 1943, (CHA 2), had a hinged door, which became the standard for the production S6s. It remained in service until 1957. (D. R. Harvey Collection)

1944, CHA 3

The Uplands Public House opened on 16 September 1932 and was closed in 2009. It stood at the junction of Sandwell Road and in front of it was where, after the closure of the Birmingham Corporation 26 tram route on 1 April 1939, the replacement number 70 bus service terminated. A brand new Corporation MCCW-bodied Leyland Titan TD6c is parked in front of the public house. CHA 3, the third SOS REC, was built in 1927 and is seen in its original condition. It is standing opposite the Uplands at the terminus of the 213 route and will shortly leave for Bearwood by way of the New Inns, Soho Station and Windmill Lane. At the rear of the bus, the original, modern-looking Carlyle B40F bodywork has a radiator panel to cool the rear-mounted engine. In 1944 it was converted to the underfloor-engined S4 and received a new Carlyle B40F body similar to that on CHA 2. (R. T. Coxon)

2579, HHA 222

At first sight, 2579, (HHA 222), looked like any other early post-war BMMO underfloor-engined bus, but it was far from that. It was built in 1946 as the one-off prototype S5. This single-decker was an integrally bodied vehicle, preceding the production S14 chassis-less buses and had a MCCW B40F body. Only the seven-bay construction and the clear, but quite small, destination box made it look different from a BMMO S6. The bus is parked in Station Street when at most two years old, with the bomb-damaged roof over New Street station awaiting its imminent demolition. (W. J. Haynes)

1947–1950: The First Post-War Single-Deckers

Background

In the 1930s, Midland Red was an early convert to oil engines with the SOS DON and SON types, which had sturdy but very lightweight bodies and yet had, by pre-war standards, a high seating capacity of usually about thirty-eight seats. Not satisfied with this, Wyndham Shire had the four advanced rear-engined REC single-deckers built during 1936 and 1937, but they were not reliable and, by the time of his retirement in April 1940, the buses were virtually out of use.

The successful wartime conversion of the four REC single-deckers to an underfloor-engined layout during the Second World War and Mr Sinclair's appointment to the newly created post of General Manager in the summer of 1944, enabled the authorisation of the building of 2579, (HHA 222) – the Metro-Cammell-bodied integral construction S5. Although the company was later to concentrate on the production of monocoque single-deckers by developing the S5 concepts HHA 222 was built on, in 1946 this was perhaps the 'bus too far'. Thus, this unique S5 concept was not pursued until 1954, when the chassisless S14 was introduced.

The early Brush and Metro-Cammell bodies never looked dated. This was a tribute to the original wartime design teams at Carlyle Road, who produced the S2-5 prototype bodies between 1942 and 1946. Their characteristically functional shape was the progenitor for 499 buses based on the same theme. Midland Red got it right the first time when they were the first manufacturer to get underfloor-engined buses into production.

Mechanically trail-blazing and well-liked by both platform and engineering departments, these early S classes played a vital part in revolutionising the post-war urban and rural Midland Red bus services.

The Pioneering Production Post–War Single–Deckers

S6

The S6s layout and style is relevant to all of the later S8 to S12 Midland Red single-deckers. The new post-war S6 featured a separate chassis and body. The 100 S6 chassis were built to the then Construction and Use width of 7 feet 6 inches and was designed to accommodate a 27 foot 6 inch body. The S6s were the only class of underfloor-engined single-decker buses to be built to this narrower width, though between 1948 and 1950 Midland Red built fifty-seven C1 and C2 coaches with Duple bodies to this width. The completed S6 bus had a smooth, straight waist railed body, although the 16-ft-long wheelbase resulted in barely 6 feet of overhang at the front and rear of the body. The chassis design followed on from the earlier prototypes with the 8.028-litre engine coupled to a four-speed constant-mesh gearbox engineered by David Brown to the requirements of Midland Red. The gearbox was quite easy to use, although, unusually, it did have a very long throw into first gear while the second, third and fourth gears had an extremely short action. It was also not uncommon for drivers to do clutchless gear changes as this was quicker than the accepted double-declutching method, following this normal practice on pre-war ZF Aphon gearboxes. The Lockheed hydraulic brakes had a single servo, which perhaps required more muscle power than on other manufacturer's products. The fanless radiator was mounted at the front of the chassis behind a full-length radiator grill, which was distinguished by the chromed radiator filler cap.

The body contract was split equally between Brush, who had been Midland Red's favoured pre-war supplier of bodies, and Metro-Cammell, who had built the integral S5. The buses looked very similar to HHA 222, but had six bays instead of seven, which gave the vehicles a much tidier appearance. There were three sliding windows on each side of the saloon and the saloon itself was trimmed in brown leather cloth, while the seats were covered in brown, fawn and orange moquette with dark brown rexine trim. Along the length of both sides of the saloon was a luggage rack and beneath them on the backs of the seats there were a variety of notices in varying styles suggesting passengers should 'take care when standing', as well as a sign stating that smoking was prohibited in the first four rows. The windscreen of the buses was recessed on the driver's side in order to avoid reflections from the saloon lights at night. The top edge of the windscreen was curved downwards and this gave the front of the buses a sad-looking appearance, which was more noticeable on the narrower S6s than on the later 8-ft-wide underfloor-engined single-deckers. At the front there was a large destination box and a separate route number indicator, while mounted in the dome at the rear there was a single-track destination box and a number blind.

The porch-style front entrance, with handrails on either side, had three steps up to the saloon and a hinged door on the bulkhead, keeping the forty forward-facing passengers warm and the platform staff 'less so'! The driver had his own external cab door but on the platform side the cab was open from waist height. The drivers of pre-war SOS buses did get some warmth from the engine, but in the underfloor-engined S6s the open nearside cab led to drivers complaining about draughts and positively Arctic driving conditions. The result was that after the first thirty S6s had been delivered, all subsequent underfloor-engined single-deckers with open porch entrances were fitted with permanent platform-side windows that could be slid open or shut.

In their original state, the S6s weighed either 2 hundred weight below or above 6½ tons with the Metro-Cammell-bodied S6 being lighter due to constructional differences that removed the need for stress panels. Additionally, the top hat section

Accles & Pollock body pillars did not employ wooden fillets and as such the exterior panels were attached with pop-rivets, which produced a much lighter structure. There were detailed external differences between those S6s bodied by Brush or MCCW, such as the front profile of the large destination box being curved outwards on the Loughborough-built bodies, while the MCCW bodies had the headlights positioned slightly lower. 3001/6-7/9-14/7/19-57/9 were all bodied by Metro-Cammell, while the balance was supplied with Brush bodywork.

Between September 1946 and July 1947, exactly 100 of these new BMMO S6 single-deckers entered service. They entered service with fleet numbers 3000–3099, but were intended to be numbered 2601–2700 – roughly following on from the last of the wartime Guy Arab II double-deckers. After the registrations, HHA 601–700 had been booked with the Smethwick registration office, it was decided to commence the post-war fleet numbers at 3000, thus creating the bus spotter's nightmare of having to take off 601 before recording the 'copped' bus.

When they first appeared in service, these buses were quite remarkable. Midland Red was still using a few single-deckers dating from 1928 and running in service with them was a fleet of these new, sleek-bodied, shiny and reliable underfloor-engined buses. It would be another three years before Leyland Motors produced their first underfloor-engined 'Olympic' HR40 single-decker and nearly four years before AEC put the prototype 'Regal' IV on the road, by which time Midland Red was operating around 500 underfloor-engined single-deck buses and fifty-seven Duple-bodied coaches with a similar chassis layout. When new, the S6s were employed on express services and even as duplicate vehicles on coach excursions, as well as their normal bus work.

When the Construction and Use Regulations were altered to allow single-deckers to be built to dimensions of 30 foot long and 8 foot wide, all the S6, S8, S9 and S10 single-deckers had their bodies extended at the rear by 1 feet 9 inches. This resulted in a body that was now 29 feet 3 inches long, which enabled the seating capacity to be increased by an extra row to a B44F layout. This unusual length meant that if the buses were lengthened to the full 30 foot length then, under the C&U Regulations, the 16-ft wheelbase would have to be lengthened as well, which would have been excessively expensive. All the S6s were lengthened by Charles Roe, increasing their weight by about four hundredweight. This rebuilding was done throughout 1953 and were the last of the Leeds-based bodybuilders' three-year contract to extend all the BMMO 27-ft 6-inch-long single-deckers. The reason for the number of seats being forty-four rather than the forty-five favoured by other operators and bodybuilders was that all Midland Red single-deckers until 1967 had centre door rear emergency exits rather than the normal location on the offside rear of the saloon.

S6s were allocated in the main away from the West Midlands, though there were always a few at Digbeth Garage. Main centres for seeing these vehicles would have been on routes operated by Hereford, Leamington, Sandacre Street in Leicester, Nuneaton, Rugby, Shrewsbury and Worcester garages. In later years, towards the end of their careers, the S6s gravitated to the more rural garages, where their 7 foot 6 inch width was well suited to trundling around narrow lanes, connecting villages to local country towns on services.

Withdrawals of the S6s began in 1961 when fifteen were taken out of service. All had gone by the end of 1964 with the exception of 3023, which survived in stock into 1965. At a time when the BET Group of bus operators was getting about thirteen years' use out of their single-deck buses, the highly innovative S6 buses managed, amazingly, between fourteen and eighteen years' service.

The 8-Foot-Wide S8, S9, S10 and S11 Single-Deck Buses

S8

The 1948 C&U Regulations increased the allowed width of buses to be 8 feet wide, enabling Midland Red to place the wider S8 into service. They were classified 'Single-deck 8-foot-wide', thus explaining why there wasn't an S7. All 100 S8s were bodied by Metro-Cammell and, except for their width, the S8 looked very similar to the S6, while mechanically they were identical to the lighter S6s, using the same BMMO 8.028-litre oil engine. The other noticeable difference was that the complete windscreen was surrounded by chrome while the nearside windscreen was not divided. The buses were numbered 3200–3299, (JHA 800–899), with 3224–3274 entering service in 1948 while the remainder arrived early in 1949. The complete batch of S8s were sent to Charles Roe for extension to B44F, with eighty-nine being modified in 1951 and the balance of eleven being attended to during 1952. In their original short-length form, the S8s weighed 6 tons 8 cwt 1 qtr, but after rebuilding they weighed in at 6 tons 13 cwt 1 qtr. 3284, (JHA 884), had a lightweight Metro-Cammell body whose unladen weight was 1 cwt under 6 tons. After severe accidents, three of the S8 class were attractively altered, receiving S15-style front ends that had electric entrance doors; 3241 was rebuilt by Carlyle in 1957 while 3217 and 3237 were similarly treated by Willowbrook in 1958. In this guise, they were designated S8 Mk 1s and were frequently used on express services. Originally the S8s were trimmed in brown leathercloth, but they were subsequently re-trimmed with red upholstery and red and magnolia leathercloth. The S8 bell-pushes were moved to the luggage rack supports, whereas those on the S6s were on the luggage rack edges.

The strangest rebuilding, possibly of any Midland Red bus, was the conversion in 1960 of 3220, (JHA 820), to 45 feet long. This was part of the campaign to get the C&U Regulations for single-deckers altered to allow buses of 36 foot length to be operated. Never to do things by halves, this bus, variously seen with either an exposed chassis extension or with a temporary green-undercoat-painted body structure, was driven to London and inspected by the Ministry of Transport. The experiment was a success as during the following year the regulations were altered and 36-ft-long single-deckers were introduced.

After Lichfield Garage's opening, over half the bus allocation was filled with S8s, and Digbeth in Birmingham always had a collection of the class. Elsewhere the class was well represented at Coalville, Hereford, Malvern, Redditch, Rugby, Stourbridge, Tamworth and Wolverhampton garages.

Withdrawals began in 1962, when twenty of the class were taken out of service, and all had gone by the end of 1965, except for the three S8 Mk 1s, which went the following year.

S9

The next 100 service buses were the S9 class and were the Brush-bodied equivalents of the Metro-Cammell S8s. Numbered 3357–3456, (LHA 357–456), these buses all entered service in 1949. The first fifty were really an 8-ft-wide version of the Brush-bodied S6 buses. The steering wheel was moved to the centre of the cab whereas on the earlier S6 and S8s they were offset in a less comfortable driving position. The first fifty had the original rear destination boxes while the second half of the batch had a single triple-track number box. The second fifty of the S9s also had modified window pans. Of the products coming out of Loughborough, the Brush bodies were typically heavier than the Metro-Cammell-bodied buses, weighing 6 tons 14 cwt 1 qtr, which went up to just under 7 tons after they were lengthened. This lengthening took place in 1952 when all of the class were extended by Charles Roe and as a consequence the seating capacity increased to B44F. 3359, (LHA 359), was fitted with a semi-automatic gearbox with two-pedal control, which was manufactured by Hobbs, who was later responsible for a hydraulic, four-speed, automatic unit being fitted to the prototype BMMO S14 4178, (THA 778). 3405, (LHA 405), was different from the rest of the S9s in that it had rubber suspension for its first two years in service and was also a trial for further developments on the integral S14 single-deckers. A large number of the S9s were allocated to Digbeth Garage as well as Tamworth but after being extended the S9s went to more rural garages such as Coalville, Malvern, Rugby, Wellington and Worcester.

One member of the batch was modified in a way that presaged future body designs. This was 3441, (LHA 441), which was rebuilt at Carlyle Road Works before it entered service. The bus had a much squarer front with a destination box that was almost flush with the roof line and a windscreen style that would be repeated on the later S13s. The bus had closing, manually operated external doors that were flat to the bodyside and these were converted to electric operation after about 1954. As a result, only a half-height internal driver's door was fitted as there was no external cab door. The bus had a half-height, low-mounted radiator grill, a front bumper and lots of 'jazzy' aluminium brightwork on the front and at waist rail-level all around the body, as well the fleet name 'MIDLAND' in raised brightwork. Designated S9 Mk 1, it was initially stationed at Bearwood Garage, but within a year was moved to Sandacre Street Garage, Leicester, where it spent the rest of its working life, being withdrawn in 1965.

Generally, Brush bodies were not as long-lived as the Metro-Cammell ones and withdrawals of the S9s began in 1962. However, despite seventy-nine being taken out of service by the end of the following year, the last two stragglers withdrawn were 3419 and 3420 in early 1967.

S10

The next batch of single-deck buses were the BMMO S10s. They were numbered 3577–3693, 3695–3702 and 3704–3732 with corresponding NHA registrations and reverted to having the body order split within the batch between Brush and Metro-Cammell. They were the last post-war single-deck buses to be built to the 27 foot 6 inch length and were mechanically the same as the S8s and S9s, except that the position of the handbrake was moved to the more conventional position of the offside of the cab. The main external difference from the previous S9 single-deckers was that all the saloon windows were fitted with sliding ventilators. In late 1949, 3577–84 and 3586–3590 were in service with the rest of the S10s becoming operational by the summer of 1950. The Metro-Cammell S10s weighed 6½ tons while the Brush examples weighed 4 cwt more. The first of all the post-war single-deckers to be extended to 29 feet 3 inches was 3600, which was completed in 1951 when the bus was barely a year old. This was the only bus to be rebuilt by Metro-Cammell, who could not accept the lucrative contract to lengthen all the S6–S11 single-deckers, having just signed the agreement to build 450 RF type single-deckers for London Transport. So the contract went to Charles Roe instead, who extended the S10s between 1952 and 1953.

3634 was fitted with an experimental BMMO 10.5-litre engine, which would first be used in a vertical form with the introduction of the D9 double-deckers. This S10 was used as a test-bed for engine development between 1952 and 1954 and again between 1955 and 1956 before reverting to the standard 8.028-litre BMMO K type engine. The drivers at Cradley Heath Garage where it spent all its re-engined time must have missed the extra power.

The S10s were generally allocated to 'town' rather than 'urban' garages, with reasonably sized allocations at Evesham, Kidderminster, Leamington, Malvern, Redditch, Swadlincote, Tamworth, Worcester, Wellington and Wolverhampton. Withdrawals began in 1956 when 3604 caught fire, but regular removals from service began with one withdrawal in 1961 and eight in the following year, while the last six went in 1966.

S11

There was just one S11, which was 3703, (NHA 703). The bus had an MCCW B40F body and entered service in 1950. It was built with independent front suspension and was another test-bed for the future S14s single-deckers. 3703 also briefly had a steering column gearchange early in its career. In 1953 the bus was extended by Roe to the B44F layout and was subsequently converted to a standard S10 by the substitution of a standard front suspension and front axle. After becoming an anonymous S10, 3703 was withdrawn in 1965.

Summary Fleet List

S6	Nos 3000–3099	HHA 601–700	Brush/MCCW B40F. Lengthened Roe B44F, 1953.	b. 1946–47 w. 1961–65
S8	Nos 3200–3299	JHA 800–899	MCCW B40F Lengthened Roe B44F, 1953. Nos. 3217, 3237 and 3241 rebuilt with S14 front.	b. 1948–49 w. 1962–65
S9	Nos 3357–3440 Nos 3442–3456	LHA 357–440 442–456	Brush B40F Lengthened Roe B44F, 1952.	b. 1949–50 w. 1962–67
S9 Mk 1	No. 3441	LHA 441	Brush B40F and rebuilt with electric doors by Carlyle, 1950. Lengthened Roe B44F, 1952.	b. 1950 w. 1963
S10	Nos 3577–3693 Nos 3695–3702 Nos 3704–3732	NHA 577–693 NHA 695–702 NHA 704–732	Brush/MCCW B40F. Lengthened Roe B44F No. 3600 1952–53. Lengthened MCCW B44F, 1951.	b.1949–50 w. 1961–66 (No. 3604) 1956
S11	No. 3703	NHA 703	MCCW B40F Lengthened Roe B44F 1953.	b. 1950 w. 1965
S12	Nos 3733–3776	NHA 733–776	Brush/MCCW B44F, 30 ft long.	b.1950–51 w. 1963–67

3002, HHA 603

The 7-feet 6-inches-wide by 27-feet 6-inches-long S6 was a dainty single-decker. It had a long 16 foot wheelbase and virtually the same amount of overhang at both ends. 3002, (HHA 603), was the second BMMO S6 to enter service in March 1947 and was allocated to Southgate Street Garage in Leicester. It had a Brush B40F body, which was painted in an all-over red livery with a thin yellow stripe and black wings. 3002 is parked on the railway bridge in London Road near Conduit Street with Leicester's railway station located behind the boarding. Its crew are killing time in front of the bus before leaving on the 639 via Great Glen and Fleckney to Saddington. (W. J. Haynes)

3009, HHA 610

3009, (HHA 610), a Metro-Cammell-bodied BMMO S6, is parked in Great Malvern during June 1952 while waiting to leave on the M27 service to Lulwall Green. It was allocated to Malvern's dormy garage, where it would remain until it was sent to Charles Roe in 1953 for lengthening. The Metro-Cammell body had its yellow strip painted slightly lower than on the Brush-bodied examples, going through the middle of the 'MIDLAND' sign above the radiator filler cap. (S. N. J. White)

3015 HHA 616

Parked outside the body shop of Charles Roe in Crossgates, Leeds, is Brush-bodied 3015 (HHA 616). When the Construction and Use Regulations were altered in 1950, all the S6 and S8–S11 single-deckers were lengthened by 1 foot 9 inches to 29 feet 3 inches. This was the maximum that buses with a 16-foot wheelbase single-decker could be lengthened to under the newly introduced legislation. At 30 feet, the prohibitive expense involved in rebuilding the wheelbase would have only given the buses an extra five seats, and so only an extra four seats were added. The new section is identifiable at the rear of the bus in the side panelling and the roof, while retaining as much of the original rear end as possible. It would return to Shrewsbury Garage, where it would stay until shortly before its withdrawal in December 1962. (S. N. J. White)

3035, HHA 636

A recently extended MCCW-bodied BMMO S6 is about to leave the stop in the St Peter's Square area outside the Shire Hall in Hereford when working on the H14 town service. By now having a B44F seating layout, somehow the delicate tapering front aspect of 3035, (HHA 636), no longer matches the extended rear end, with the elongated rearmost side window looking out of balance with the rest of the bus. (Southdown Enthusiasts)

3061, HHA 662

On 18 October 1962, 3061, (HHA 662), a Brush B44F-bodied BMMO S6, stands in the temporary bus station in Moor Street, Birmingham. It is working on the 166 route to Marston Green via Coventry Road and Sheldon, which crossed the boundary into Warwickshire and could, therefore, pick up and set down passengers inside the city without restriction. In the background, the original Bull Ring Centre was still under construction and Moor Street station was still being used by steam-hauled suburban trains. Today, only the Edwardian railway station remains, while the huge, revolutionary 1960s shopping centre was replaced by the Bull Ring Centre, which opened in 2003. (W. Ryan)

3220, JHA 820
The strangest rebuilding of a Midland Red bus was the conversion in 1960 of 3220, (JHA 820). This was temporally lengthened to 45 feet as part of the campaign to get the Construction and Use Regulations for single-deckers altered to allow the operation of 36-foot-long buses. 3220 was trialled with either an exposed chassis extension, as in this case when parked in Carlyle Road Works yard, or with a temporary green-undercoat-painted, windowless body structure. (D. R. Harvey Collection)

3236, JHA 836
In June 1948, BMMO S8 3236, (JHA 836), fully equipped with Bearwood destination blinds, has just been delivered to Bearwood Garage and has yet to enter service. The red paintwork positively gleams in the summer sunshine and the whole look of the bus is helped by the subtle, yellow-coloured lining out. Being 8 feet wide, the extra width allows for the frontal appearance of the curved windscreen to be less doleful than the narrower S6s. (W. J. Haynes)

3241, JHA 841

Three S8 single-deckers, 3217, 3237 and 3241, were involved in serious accidents and were rebuilt with S15 front ends. 3241, along with 3217, was rebuilt by Willowbrook with electrically-operated jack-knife doors and with a re-moquetted interior, which made for a most attractive bus. 3241, (JHA 841), turns into Rea Street from Digbeth in Birmingham, before turning right into Digbeth coach station. Although not quite a dual-purpose vehicle, it was used on express services and is seen here halfway along the long route between Northampton and Shrewsbury via Birmingham on the X96. (L. Mason)

3258, JHA858

3247, (JHA847), a MCCW-bodied BMMO S8, is parked in Digbeth Garage yard soon after being extended by Roe to B44F capacity. It still carries the first style of shaded fleet number and a thin straw livery band. The S8s were fitted with horizontal BMMO 8.028-litre engines and were capable of undertaking long stage carriage duties, as well as suburban routes such as the 166 service to Marston Green via Coventry Road. Although lacking luggage boots, they had more than adequate parcel racks in the saloon for parcel-laden shoppers. (S. N. J. White)

3259, JHA 859

The Midland Red bus shelters were of the utilitarian corrugated iron variety, with black and white-painted scaffolding poles, and afforded the waiting passengers no more than a token of protection. Passengers load onto 3259, (JHA 859), whose saloon would be a much more comfortable proposition than standing in the cold late afternoon sunshine near the Kings Head in Hagley Road West, Bearwood. This extended Metro-Cammell-bodied BMMO S8 is working on the 190 route from Birmingham to Bridgnorth via Halesowen, Stourbridge, Kinver and Enville – a journey of nearly two hours. (A. D. Broughall)

3370, LHA 370

3370, (LHA 370), is parked in Banbury town centre in the shadow of the row of Georgian buildings, having arrived in the town on the 514 service from Claydon (some 6 miles to the north and just over the border in Northamptonshire). This Brush-bodied BMMO S9 is in an interim state, having been extended by Roe, with the longer rear side saloon window, but is still painted with black wings, a thin straw lining-out band below the windows and a thick, shaded fleet number. (A. D. Packer)

3386, LHA 386

The BMMO S9 was really just an 8-foot-wide Brush-bodied version of the S6. It had polished metal sliding saloon ventilators, a straight-sided front destination box, slightly shorter guttering at the front of the driver's cab and higher-set headlights. 3386, (LHA 386), which had entered service in April 1949, stands in Station Street when about to work on the once-a-day departure of the 347 service to Alcester via Wythall and Studley, which left Birmingham at 2 p.m. It is parked in the shadow of the arched roof of New Street station, which was demolished later the same year, having been structurally weakened by bomb blasts during air raids in 1940 and 1941. (W. J. Haynes)

3400, LHA 400

Dudley bus station was partly built on the steep hill in Birmingham Street, which is where 3400, (LHA 400), has just arrived. This Brush-bodied BMMO S9 had been at Dudley Garage since February 1952 and was lengthened to become a B44F single-decker during the same year. It is going to travel to Blackheath via the steep Portway route, taking the service over the Sedgley-Northfield Ridge, which, as the main watershed in the Midlands, necessitated some long, arduous ascents and descents. (A. D. Broughall)

3416, LHA 416

S9s 3357–3406 had full-width rear destination boxes, but the rest of the class had number-only destination boxes in the rear dome. 3416, (LHA 416), is in Brush's Loughborough factory immediately prior to delivery in June 1949. The Brush-bodied buses could always be distinguished from MCCW-bodied vehicles by the straight-sided front destination box. Within three years it would be extended to 29 feet 3 inches by Roe to a B44F layout and would remain in service until 1963. (Brush)

3441, LHA 441

3441, (LHA 441), stands on the Abbey Street, Leicester, bus park. It was the only S9 Mk 1 and was nicknamed the 'American S9' and was new in June 1950. 3441 was rebuilt before entering service with a modified flat front similar to the later S13s and lots of aluminium bright work around the body at waist rail level. The bus had a half-height, low-mounted radiator grill and a front bumper. It entered service in June 1950 and was initially allocated to Bearwood Garage. After assessment, it went to Sandacre Street, where it spent the rest of its life until withdrawal in September 1963, having been extended to B44F layout by Charles H. Roe, Leeds. (M. Rooum)

3454, LHA 454

3454, (LHA 454) is seen working along Barker Street when on the S13 Shrewsbury town service on 25 August 1960. This Brush-bodied BMMO S9 entered service in November 1949 and, from February 1951 until its withdrawal in May 1963, was always a Shrewsbury bus. The car park on the left has in it an Austin A30 two-door saloon, a Ford Anglia 100E and a Vauxhall Twelve-Four saloon. In the distance, another Midland Red single-decker is leaving the Bridge Street bus station. The large half-timbered Tudor building is in the Mardol, an area linking the edge of the medieval Shrewsbury and the River Severn. (R. F. Mack)

3595, NHA 595

There were 154 single-deck BMMO S10s. They were fitted with horizontal BMMO K type 8.028-litre engines, which were underfloor-mounted, and had B40F bodywork built to BMMO design by either Brush or Metro-Cammell. 3595, (NHA 595), was new in January 1950 and had a B40F body built by MCCW. In its unrebuilt state, the tyres looked somehow larger and more purposeful. It has been working on the 617 route to Syston and is standing in the bus station at St Margaret's in about 1951, two years after it was lengthened by Charles Roe. (W. J. Haynes)

3606, NHA 606

3606, (NHA 606), a Brush-bodied BMMO S10 that is by now a forty-four-seater, is loading up at the 586 stop in Coventry's Pool Meadow bus station, where it will shortly depart for its home town of Rugby, via Brandon. The yellow lining-out below the windscreen was retained after the bus was lengthened but it was eliminated in mid-1955. The fleet numbers were still in yellow and shaded in black, but these too were replaced in early 1956. 3606 entered service in April 1950 from Rugby Garage and would remain there until March 1964. (M. Hayhoe)

3686, NHA 686

Above: Awaiting its crew while parked in Nuneaton bus station is 3686, (NHA 686). It is 1963 and as the distant new Leyland Leopard bus leaves the bus station, the slightly down-at-heel Metro-Cammell-bodied BMMO S10 is beginning to look its age. It would be withdrawn the following March. The bus has the simplified spray-painted all-over red livery without any other colours to replace the yellow lining-out and the black-painted wings of the previous livery. (A. D. Broughall)

3674, NHA 674

Opposite below: Loading up with passengers while employed on the 900 service from Wellington to St George's, is a recently extended Brush-bodied BMMO S10, 3674, (NHA 674). The bus is in Market Street, Oakengates, in around 1955 and is standing just beyond the former Great Western Railway bridge, near the town's railway station. New in June 1950 to Wellington Garage, 3674 was withdrawn in September 1965, having spent its entire operational life working in this industrial area in East Shropshire. (Temple Press)

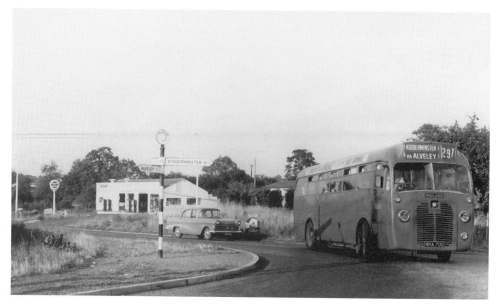

3700, NHA 700

Sandwiched between the prototype S13, 3694, and the only S11 was a small batch of eight BMMO S10s. 3700, (NHA 700), one of four bodied by Metro-Cammell, turns off the A442, just south of the unusually named hamlet of Quatt. It is going to the small former coal-mining village of Alveley on the east side of the River Severn while being used on the 297 route from Bridgnorth to Kidderminster. The Vauxhall Victor's still unrusted bodywork would date this view to around the early 1960s. (R. F. Mack)

3712, NHA 712

Above: When New Street station opened in 1854, it had the largest single-span iron and glass roof in the world. *Bradshaw's Guide* wrote that, 'The semicircular roof is 1,100 feet long, 205 feet wide and 80 feet high, composed of iron and glass and without the slightest support except that afforded by the pillars on either side.' Alas, after the Second World War, the roof showed the awful effects of wartime bombing and was quickly demolished. A BMMO S10 with a Brush body in its original condition stands in Queens Drive, Birmingham, when just one year old, in 1951. It operated for two years before being extended by Roe, thus increasing its seating capacity by four to a B44F layout. 3712, (NHA 712), waits in front of 3409, (LHA 409), a 1949 BMMO S9, which would also be lengthened in 1952. (S. N. J. White)

3703, NHA 703

Opposite below: 3703, (NHA 703), had standard MCCW B40F bodywork and was indistinguishable from an S10, except for the slightly canted front wheels. Put into service as the unique S11, it had prototype independent front suspension and it was then fitted with standard suspension in 1957, which it retained until it was withdrawn in July 1965. It is working on the 136 route from Romsley, high in the Clent Hills, through Hunnington (then the home of Bluebird Toffee) and Halesowen before heading to either Bearwood or on to Birmingham. The bus has been extended but still retained its independent front suspension. (G. Davies)

3717, NHA 717

New in July 1950, Metro-Cammell-bodied BMMO S10 3717, (NHA 717), is carrying a full complement of passengers as it approaches Victoria coach station in Buckingham Palace Road from Birmingham. Even when middle-aged, these service buses were still used as duplicates for coach services. With the driver's internal cab screen and the saloon door closed, these buses gave a comfortable, draught-free ride, and on journeys such as these, the full-length luggage racks were a real boon. Behind it is a 1954 Willowbrook C37C-bodied BMMO C3 coach, 4203, (UHA 203). (R. H. G. Simpson)

3774, NHA 774

3774, (NHA 774), is still in its original lined-out livery when standing in the temporary Abbey Street parking lot opposite St Margaret's bus station in Leicester. It has arrived in the city from Grantham and Melton Mowbray on the 661 service, which served the north-east limits of Midland Red's operating area. It is parked alongside a wartime Guy Arab, whose body had been rebuilt by Brush. (D. R. Harvey Collection)

Heavyweight 30-Foot Single-Deckers

S12

There were just forty-four S12 single-deckers, which were numbered 3733–3776, (NHA 733–776), and of which twenty-three entered service in 1950. On the first day of the change to permitting 30-ft-long single-deckers to operate in service in the UK, the first S12 was in service and the class was, therefore, forty-four-seater from new, although realistically these buses were part of the S10 contract. The body contract was split between Brush and Metro-Cammell, but despite the increase in the legal length – as with the buses that were to be extended over the next two years – the S12s were built as 29-ft 3-inch-long saloons so that the standard production 16 inch wheelbase could be retained. The Brush bodies, delivered between September 1950 and July 1951, weighed 6 tons 19½ cwt unladen while the Elmdon product was once again considerably lighter at 6 tons 14¾ cwt. S12 3734, (NHA 734), was equipped with an AEC 9.6-litre engine from 1951 until 1958 and similar bus 3763, (NHA 763), ran with a Leyland 0.600 engine during the same period.

All the Metro-Cammell-bodied S12 had their sliding windows painted red while the Brush ones had for the first time the much-improved stainless steel ones, until the mid-1950s when spray-booth painting got to them! Withdrawals began in 1964 and all had gone by 1967. With the withdrawal of S12s 3761 and 3762, the last of the first generation of Midland Red single-deckers with separate chassis and bodies had gone some twenty years since the first S6s came on the road.

The S12s were the last of the first generation 30-ft-long BMMO single-deckers. They were the ultimate underfloor-engined vehicles built with separate chassis and a seating capacity of forty-four whose lineage could be traced back to the prototype S2.

The S13, S14 and S15 single-deckers maintained the Midland Red family resemblance, which was derived from the wartime rebuilt REC chassis. The groundbreaking 100 S6s of 1946 and 1947 were little more than tidied-up versions of the S2, S3 and S4, while the next major advance was the introduction of the 8-ft-wide S8–S11 buses, which again put Midland Red at the forefront of the operation of the wider vehicle format.

The S13s was something of a 'half-way house' in the development of the shorter-length S type BMMO buses. They were constructed to the new 30 foot length, which had been introduced on 1 June 1950 and represented a new venture in certain aspects of the body design, but they were the last Midland Red single-deckers to have separate chassis and bodies. They were almost exclusively built as dual-purpose vehicles, thereby representing a new style of vehicle for the company. The integral, or chassis-less, S14 and S15s were related in shape but differed in function, with the S14s being a mechanically advanced, but extremely basically bodied, no-frills service bus while the S15 was the dual-purpose successor to the S13s. The construction of the S13, S14 and S15 single-deckers was spread over twelve years from 1950 until 1962, which, coincidentally, was the approximate intended lifespan of these vehicles.

S13 Mk 1

3694 (NHA 694)

The first BMMO single-decker built to the new 30 foot x 8 foot dimensions was 3694, (NHA 694). It entered service on 1 June 1950, which was the first day this legislation came into operation. 3694 was the solitary S13 Mk 1 and had a Brush-built body that was mounted for the first time on the new 17 foot 6 inch wheelbase chassis, dropping the original 16 inch wheelbase length. Like all the subsequent S13s, it had the standard horizontal 8.028-litre engine coupled to the usual David Brown-manufactured constant-mesh gearbox.

The new, longer wheelbase restored the proportions of the original-length S6s and S8 to S11s. The lengthened single-decker S13 Mk 1 design looked to be a much more balanced vehicle. The Brush body had a capacity of forty-four and its trim and styling was similar to that of the earlier S9 Mk 1, 3441, (LHA 441), which was built in March 1950 but to the old 27 foot 6 inch length.

Mr Sinclair had been involved in discussions within the bus industry to improve and set standards for the new generation of underfloor-engined single-decker body designs. The fruit of Mr Sinclair's work was the 'Americanisation' of both 3441 and the newly introduced, longer S13 Mk 1 – both of which had chromed front bumpers and three strips of brightwork below the saloon windows at waist rail level. Ironically, despite this pioneering work, Midland Red was to remain outside the subsequent BET underfloor engine single-deckers body styles built by Weymann, Park Royal and Willowbrook for many years, who owed a lot to these early manoeuvres in bus bodywork standardisation.

The front destination box was incorporated into the dome on 3694 and was fitted with electric doors, a neat two-piece windscreen losing the 'frowning' appearance of the earlier single-deckers and was bestowed with a separate driver's cab door. The driver had his own half-height door from the platform and, unlike all previous and subsequent Midland Red-built S type single-deckers, the S13s did not have a full-height partition behind the driving position. The lengthened saloon meant that there were six saloon windows instead of five, each one having sliding ventilators, while a small window was set on the side at the rear of the body.

3694, known as *The Queen Mary*, presumably because of the tenuous cross-Atlantic links, acted as the pre-production prototype for the S13s. It spent virtually all of its life working from Cradley Heath Garage alongside a number of other experimental buses and was finally withdrawn in June 1964.

S13 Mk 2 Prototypes

3877 (OHA877)

The first of the three prototype S13 Mk 2s was 3877, (OHA 877). This bus entered service in February 1951 and was bodied 'in-house' by Carlyle on Metal Sections frames. This Oldbury-based company was to become the main supplier of body frames to Midland Red and this bus was the first supplied to incorporate their framework. 3877 had a rather plain-looking forty-four-seat bus body, which used a lot of Brush components and even had a full-length standard S12-style radiator grill. 3877 was equipped with an experimental gearbox with synchromesh on its third and fourth gears and was the only S13 to have manually driver-operated doors, using a handle that could easily be mistaken by the uninitiated for the gear change lever. It was initially allocated to Cradley Heath Garage, working on the Birmingham to Gornal Wood route, or on Brierley Hill or Halesowen services. 3877 spent most of its later working life operating from Leamington Garage, although for its last months it was back in the Black Country, allocated to Dudley Garage, where its non-standard, thin, short-backed seats didn't matter as much on short urban services. Despite all these non-standard features, 3877 remained in service until 1966.

3878 (OHA 878)

The second S13 Mk 2 to enter service in August 1951 was bodied by Willowbrook, who in 1950 and 1951 was involved with the rebuilding of some thirty-two wartime bodies mounted on Daimler CWA6s. 3878, (OHA 878), was the only new Willowbrook body purchased by Midland Red, until the 1962 order for sixty-five Leyland Leopard PSU3/4Rs.

The distinctive body had typical Willowbrook window panes, which had square corners at the top of each saloon window bay, except for the first window, whose forward edge had a curved radius that incorporated the sliding ventilator. This bus was also a forty-four-seater and could also be easily recognised by the extremely narrow front entrance crowned by a low weather shield. It also had a unique driver's-side window with a small rubber-mounted signalling window below the main cabside window. 3878 was also recognisable by its half-sized, horizontal-slatted radiator grill, which spoilt an otherwise pleasant-looking bus. 3878 was allocated in its early years to Cradley Heath Garage and spent most of its later life based at Hereford Garage, where it survived until 1967.

3879 (OHA 879)

The final 1951 prototype S13 was 3879, (OHA 879). This was a dual-purpose forty-seat vehicle that was designed for the long limited-stop X-services, stand-in excursion work and for normal stage carriage bus operation. The Carlyle-assembled body used parts supplied by Brush. The completed vehicle, with its almost coach-standard seats, had slightly more curved bodywork below the waist rail. The half-height radiator grill was a distinctly tidier affair than that fitted to 3878 and was the direct ancestor of the type employed on the S14s, except for an untidy vertical chrome bar.

3879 was initially allocated to Digbeth Garage in August 1951 and was, like many of the production S13s, well suited to worked on the long Express services centred on Birmingham, such as the X68 route to Coventry and Leicester, the X72 to Cheltenham and Gloucester and the long X96 route linking Shrewsbury and Wellington in the west with Wolverhampton and Birmingham, before travelling eastward to Coventry, Rugby and Northampton (where a one-way trip took five hours and twenty-five minutes). 3879 was the first of the three prototype S13s to be withdrawn, being taken out of service in 1964.

Production S13 Mk 2s

3880–3975

The production batch of S13 Mk 2s was numbered 3880–3975, (OHA 880–975). All of the production S13s were fitted with the usual 8.028-litre horizontal engine coupled to the standard David Brown constant-mesh gearbox via a single-plate clutch. The braking system was a Lockheed hydraulic type with a servo pump and this combination remained standard throughout the lives of the S13 dual-purpose single-deckers, with one exception. This was 3960, (OHA 960), which was experimentally fitted with disc brakes on the front and rear wheels in 1952 as part of the development programme for the S14s.

Of the batch of ninety-five vehicles, the body contract was split between Brush, who built fifty bodies on 3880–3907/29–31/3–50 and 3952 and Nudd Brothers & Lockyer of Kegworth, who built the remaining forty-five. Between 1949 and 1951, Nudd Brothers had dealings with Midland Red by rebuilding a considerable number of pre-war SOS SON single-deckers. Brush, who had initially won the order for all ninety-five of the S13 single-deckers, ceased bodybuilding in the spring of 1952 so the balance of the order went to this small and largely unheard of bodybuilder, who by the end of the year had been taken over by Duple, becoming somewhat unimaginatively titled Duple (Midland). The first S13, were delivered to Midland Red in February 1952 from Brush, while the last two Brush-bodied S13s, 3950 and 3952, were completed in June 1952.

The DP40F bodies produced by the two companies did have considerable differences. The Nudd Brothers-bodied buses weighed a fraction over 7 tons while the Brush bodies were some five hundredweight more. The most readily identified feature between the two bodybuilders was that the Brush bodies had a raised moulding about 6 inches deep below the windscreen. Within this moulding were the two side lights, the illuminated 'MIDLAND' sign and a pair of small, rectangular ventilation grills. Beneath this was the normal full-length grill that was fitted to all the production S13 Mk 2s, with the exception of the Nudd-bodied 3955, which initially had a half-height chromed horizontally slatted grill that would reappear on the prototype S14, 4178, (THA 778). Several other standard S13s, including 3914 and 3958, were also fitted with an S14-style grill.

The Nudd bodies had a plain front panel and the side lights were mounted in a lower position, level with the top of the radiator grill panel. Another distinguishing feature was in the front dome, where the Nudd Brothers body had a less-integrated destination box than the Brush-bodied version. In common with all previous post-war S type single-deckers, these 30-foot-long S13s were equipped with a central rear emergency door. Above this, set into the rear dome, was the standard Midland Red triple number destination box.

With their high-backed semi-coach seats, open plan interiors and heavyweight construction, the S13s were ideal vehicles for the X services, as duplicates to Victoria Coach Station in London, for private hire duties and for the odd excursion to the seaside, where the S13s loved to frolic and play on the beaches! With the exception of 3919, all were repainted into the coach livery of red with a black roof in 1956. They remained on these duties for around ten years, with most garages each having a small allocation. They only started to relinquish this role, to be demoted to bus work, when the second batch of S15s was introduced in 1962.

The S13 odd man out was 3919, (OHA 919). In the early 1950s, a number of operators began carrying out experiments with standee single-deckers. Midland Red were keen to develop such a vehicle and, accordingly, 3919, a Nudd Brothers-bodied S13, was not placed into service but was immediately altered at Carlyle Road Works to a front and rear door B32D layout with ten single seats on the nearside and a reduced number of normal seats in the offside of the body. This left a good deal of floor space within the body for twenty-eight strap-hanging passengers and with more space for further standees around the rear exit doors, which were a slightly modified set of S13s front doors. 3919, in common with virtually all other contemporary single-deck buses built to this layout, was given the unflattering soubriquet of 'cattle truck'. The bus was operated by Leamington and Shrewsbury garages but the layout was not popular, resulting in its conversion in 1954 to, uniquely, a single-door B44F bus.

In 1956, all ninety-five dual-purpose S13 Mk 2s, including 3879, were repainted in the simplified coach livery of the time with a black roof. Almost at the end of their lives, a number of S13s were equipped with coach seats from the redundant C3 coaches whose Willowbrook bodies were being replaced.

The S13s were the last of the real heavyweight post-war S type single-deckers. They gave a solid and comfortable ride even if their top-end performance was a little lacking for excursion work. They were taken out of service between 1964 and 1967, with many reverting to the all-over red livery towards the end of their lives.

3733, NHA 733

Parked in Bradford Street, Birmingham, just beyond Mill Street at the back of Digbeth coach station, is 3733, (NHA 733). In around 1959, this Brush-bodied BMMO S12 is about to work on the 158 route to Coventry via Solihull and Hampton-in-Arden from Birmingham's Bull Ring. This BMMO S12 was the first Midland Red single-decker to be fitted from new with 29 foot 3 inch bodywork, and entered service in September 1950. The S12s were some of the first single-deckers of this length to enter service in the UK, as the legislation had only been passed two months previously. (A. D. Broughall)

3743, NHA 743

Above: In company with one of Barton's wonderful front entrance Duple-bodied Leyland Titan PD1As, 3743, (NHA 743), is in Mount Street bus station in Nottingham. New in October 1950, this BMMO S12 had a Metro-Cammell B44F body. Passengers are seen disembarking from the single-decker, having just arrived from Birmingham via Tamworth and Ashby on the X99 long-distance express service in 1954. This journey was timed at two hours and forty-five minutes and shows just how versatile these early post-war underfloor-engined single-deckers were. (G. H. F. Atkins)

3694, NHA 694

Opposite below: In 1952, Cradley Heath Garage, which also had extensive repair facilities, had an open day and exhibited some of the latest buses in the Midland Red fleet. 3694, (NHA 694), was the solitary Mk 1 BMMO S13 prototype and had, for the first time, 30-foot-long B44F Brush bodywork. It was fitted with a modified S9 Mk 1 front, which was first developed on 3441, an aluminium trim and power doors before entering service. New in May 1950, it ran road trials from 1 June 1950, before entering service the following September from Cradley Heath Garage. The body on 3694 had the extra small bay at the rear of the saloon rather than the long bay found on all the extended buses. It was withdrawn in June 1964. (D. R. Harvey Collection)

3877, OHA 877

After the success with 3693, three further developmental BMMO S13s were constructed and were known as Mk 2s. The first of the three S13 Mk 2 prototype BMMO S13 buses was built in February 1951 and its B44F body was assembled by Carlyle using Metal Section body frames and was finished using Brush parts. 3877 had rather short-backed, uncomfortable and upright bus seats with thin cushions, but this didn't matter so much on the short urban services it was mainly used on. 3877, (OHA 877), is parked in Pool Meadow bus station's parking area in Coventry, having arrived on the 517 service. It was at Leamington Garage until late 1965 and was withdrawn in August 1966. (D. R. Harvey Collection)

3878, OHA 878

Entering service in August 1951, 3878, (OHA 878), the second of the S13 Mk 2s, was fitted with a B44F Willowbrook body to BMMO design. Willowbrook had never been a supplier of new bus bodies to Midland Red but was at the time renovating the wartime Daimler CWA6s. 3878, (OHA 878), had square top corners just like the Willowbrook rebuilt wartime buses. It also had an extremely narrow front entrance, which slowed up loading, and a distinctively deep weather shield above the doors. It was fitted with a most undistinguished, small, horizontally slotted radiator grill. The bus is filling up with passengers at the 136 bus stop in Navigation Street, Birmingham, when about to leave for Romsley via Halesowen. 3878 was withdrawn in March 1967. (J. Cull)

3879, OHA 879

The only one of the S13 Mk 2 prototypes to be fitted out as a dual-purpose vehicle was 3879, (OHA 879). The DP40F bodywork was built at Carlyle Works using parts almost entirely from Brush and was noted for its comfortable seats. It had a pre-production S14 radiator grill, with a rather unnecessary central chrome strip. In 1956 it was repainted in the latest red coach livery with a black roof. It was involved in an accident on 14 October 1964 and was withdrawn two months later. It is parked when brand new with the BMMO LA in Central Works' yard. (R. F. Mack)

3919, OHA 919

The BMMO S13s odd man out was 3919, (OHA 919). This Nudd Brothers-bodied example was rebuilt at Carlyle Road Works before entering service to a front and rear door layout with ten rows of single seats on the nearside and a reduced number of normal seats in the offside of the body. Midland Red was keen to develop and trial such a standee single-decker. The B32D layout had room for another twenty-eight strap-hanging standees in the saloon and around the rear exit doors, which were a slightly modified set of S13 front doors. The bus was tried out at several garages, including working on Leamington town services, and is parked in front of that town's Midland Red garage. It was not popular and was converted to a single-door vehicle in 1954 but, uniquely for the batch of production S13s, was equipped as B44F. (D. R. Harvey Collection)

3928, OHA 928

On Sunday, 9 May 1965, 3928, (OHA 928), a Nudd DP40F-bodied BMMO S13, stands in front of the splendid Queen's Hotel in Stephenson Street, which survived until it was closed on New Year's Eve 1965. The Austin FX4 taxi is parked at what was originally the location of highly decorative wrought-iron railings and a line of trees, which separated the original horse carriage drive from Stephenson Street. Parked in front of the colonnades in front of the hotel, the two dual-purpose single-deckers are, as the date suggests, undertaking a rail replacement service at a time when the original New Street station was being reconstructed. (D. R. Harvey Collection)

3955, OHA 955

Above: Two of the BMMO S13s were fitted with S14-type radiator grills in 1963. These transformed the appearance of both 3914, (OHA 914), and 3955, (OHA 955). With its Nudd Brothers & Lockyer DP40F body painted in the 1956 dual-purpose livery, at first sight it might have been mistaken for a later S15 single-decker. Easily recognised as a Nudd-built body by the slightly lower front side lights, 3955 is parked at the rear of Bearwood Garage in company with a very smart, black-painted Morris Oxford Mk V saloon. (A. D. Broughall)

3952, OHA 952

Opposite below: Parked in the railway yard in company with some 'blood and custard'-liveried railway carriages at Banbury railway station in 1956 is 3952, (OHA 952). This BMMO S13 – by now in the red and black coach livery – was the last of the fifty bodied by Brush with a DP40F seating layout. It entered service in May 1952 and had the dubious distinction of being the last single-deck vehicle to leave the Loughborough-based coachbuilder, with only two trolleybuses for Nottingham City Transport following it. (P. Kingston)

Lightweight 30-Foot Single-Deckers

LA

The next underfloor-engined Midland Red was a throwback to the prototype S5 of 1946: 2579, (HHA 222), which was an integral, chassis-less single-decker. The necessity to get the new S6s into service and then build up the post-war fleet's strength rather put the integral BMMO single-decker on the 'back burner', so it was not until 1951 that work began on the only LA to be built. This bus, numbered 3977, (OHA 977), was a half-way house – a test-bed for new ideas following on from 2579 and the precursor to the prototype S14 4178, (THA 778), which perhaps might have been better designated the LA Mk 2, as it had only a vague resemblance to the many production S14s.

3977 was, numerically at least, the hundredth S13, but structurally it could have hardly have been more different. It was a chassisless forty-four-seater whose Carlyle body was built using a large a mount of aluminium – thus the LA nomenclature referring to its light alloy construction. It superficially resembled an S13 but looked more like a body built by Saunders-Roe.

The LA was the third Midland Red single-decker to have bright alloywork on the body with a thick prominent rubbing strip at the floor level, which also bisected the headlights on the front panel. The half-height radiator grill had twelve chromed horizontal bars, which looked better than the effort put on 3878, while there was a decorative single strip of polished aluminium bodywork below the saloon windows. The LA had the same 17 foot 6 inch wheelbase as the S13s but was dimensionally slightly different at 29 feet 11 inches long and 7 feet 11 inches wide. It retained the B44F layout, yet the bus weighed only 5 tons 18 cwt. 3977 had independent front suspension and torsional rubber-mounted rear suspension, and was fitted with the still-experimental 10.5-litre lightweight aluminium horizontal BMMO engine de-rated to 120 bhp, which was similar to the unit experimentally fitted to S10 3634.

After running trials from Carlyle Road Works carrying sandbags and shadowing service buses, the LA was ready in April 1952, but the engineering staff at Cradley Heath Garage had a total rethink about the engine. At a stroke, the bus was changed from what must have been a somewhat lively performer into a somewhat underpowered vehicle, being equipped with a Leyland 0.350 engine of 5.76 litres that was obviously installed to assess a small engine coupled to a lightweight single-decker. To use an old First World War soldier's expression, 'It went from the sublime to the gor blimey!' Further engine experiments were undertaken during the vehicle's operational life, which saw 3977 spending long periods either over the pits in Cradley Heath Garage (from where it operated during its first three service years) or back at Carlyle Road Works. The bus was worked very hard when it was used by the Carlyle Road Test Department, having been pounded around the Belgian pavé track at Mira near Nuneaton. As a result, when it started work on services such as Cradley Heath's 138 route, the body rattled and vibrated as if it was nearing the end of its life! In 1955, it was sent to Wellington Garage in Shropshire and initially kept its Leyland engine until 1956, whereupon it went back to the big BMMO 10.5-litre engine for another year in order to test out the hills in the Shrewsbury and Ironbridge area. Finally, in 1957, it was fitted with a standard 8.028-litre BMMO horizontal engine, which it retained until its premature storage in early 1960 before being finally withdrawn in December 1961 after failing its CoF Test, due to the appalling state of the lightweight body work.

OTC 738

One bus built by Saunders-Roe was OTC 738, a prototype Leyland Tiger Cub PSUC1/1 with a B44F body. It was demonstrated in 1951 purely for comparison purposes to Midland Red and was used on the Birmingham to Kingswinford 138 service operating from Cradley Heath Garage. It was fitted with a Leyland 0.350 5.76 litre engine coupled to a constant-mesh gearbox and had a non-standard air-brakes. The bus was the first of the two Tiger Cub Leyland Motors demonstrators and was sold to Llynfi Motors of Maesteg.

S14 Prototypes

In 1954, the culmination of the work with the S5 and LA chassisless single-deckers was the new S14 model. 4178, (THA 778), was the prototype and had every new experimental feature possible available. As with the S5 and the LA, 4178 was a chassis-less single-decker and had independent front suspension retaining wishbone linkages using Metalastick rubber components, while the rear suspension used the same toggle-link rear suspension that had first been employed on the LA. The bus had Girling disc brakes on both axles, which had been experimentally tested on S13 3960 in 1952, and a disc transmission handbrake. The rear axle only had a single pair of tyres – a feature redolent of 1920s single-deckers. The latest KL development of the new BMMO 8.028-litre horizontal engine was used, which was coupled to a Hobbs fully-automatic epicyclic gearbox with hydraulically operated friction clutches that selected the necessary ratio for the road conditions. THA 778 had the same 17 foot 6 inch wheelbase as fitted to the previous 30-ft-long wheelbase single-deckers.

The lightweight six-bay integral construction body used Metal Section steel frames with light alloy panelling and the unladen weight of the bus was an amazingly low 4 tons 18 cwt. 4178 had a B44F layout with electrically operated, driver-controlled entrance doors. The windscreen design was unique to the prototype, which, although similar to the S13s, retained the inset opening top half for the driver. The frontal design was very similar to the Nudd Brothers & Lockyer S13s, though the front destination boxes were fitted into a flat face. The slatted horizontal radiator grill was similar to the one on S13 3955 but with a chromed cap set into a V-shaped recess. 4178, at its lowest weight, scaled just 5 tons ½ cwt.

The bus was rebuilt with a standard production S14 front end, which was only a subtle change, but with a new windscreen and standard front grill it almost looked like a production S14, though the long wheelbase always gave it away. In 1954 the Hobbs gearbox was replaced with a standard David Brown constant-mesh one and in 1958 it was altered to B40F and one-man operation. 4178 spent its early years working on Smethwick local bus services from Bearwood Garage before moving to Digbeth, and later spent its declining years at Wellington Garage. This innovative bus was taken out of service in January 1967.

The second S14 was the pre-production prototype 4254, (UHA 254), which also entered the fleet in December 1954. 4254 was more of an introductory S14 than a prototype, having a number of non-standard features to the rest of the batch. It was initially allocated to Digbeth, which was close enough to Carlyle Road so that remedial treatment could be given. It was another chassis-less vehicle with independent front suspension, a Hobbs Phase 3 automatic gearbox and a 17 foot 6 inch wheelbase. A standard four-speed gearbox was fitted in 1960. It was withdrawn in November 1967.

S14 Production Vehicles

The intended S14 construction programme was originally for 269 vehicles, but between 1955 and 1958 only 218 S14 single-deckers, in three batches, were placed in service. These were 4255–4352, (UHA 254–352), built between April 1955 and June 1956, with those after 4329 entering service during 1956. The chassis-less-construction S14s had the same type of independent front suspension as the two prototype vehicles, but were fitted with a standard four-speed constant-mesh manual David Brown gearbox and were built with shorted 16 foot 4 inch wheelbases. They retained the new KL 8.028-litre BMMO engine, but in common with many of these engines, suffered from reliability problems, with blown head gaskets being a regular problem, which was easily identifiable by oil stains leaking through the lower panels and rusty water marks on the radiator grill. The bodywork was constructed on Metal Section frames in Oldbury and was glazed, panelled and trimmed by BMMO at the Central Works in Carlyle Road. Two of the S14s had experimental engines, with 4310 being fitted with an AEC 7.685 engine, which it retained until 1966, while 4347 received a Rootes TS3 3.26-litre two-stroke engine coupled to a five-speed gearbox.

The second batch, numbered 4553–4600, (553–600 AHA), were the first Midland Red buses to have reverse registrations. All entered service between April 1956 and February 1957 with 4553/65/ 90 and 96–4600 all being 1957 deliveries. 4573 ran with a Leyland o.350 5.76 engine until 1958. The final batch was numbered 4651–4721, (651–2 AHA and 653–721 BHA). It took two years to place these in service, with 4651–75 arriving from February 1957, those up to 4718 being received throughout 1958, and the last three coming in May 1959. Fifty of the intended S14s were built as the upgraded S15 dual-purpose single-deckers in 1957. There was to have been a 269th S14, which would have been 4722, but once the body frame had been completed the skeletal vehicle was redesigned and became the revolutionary prototype BMMO C5 coach, registered 722 BHA.

Uniquely, the destination number box on the S14s was placed on the offside of the front dome. There were numerous differences between the prototype and the production S14 vehicles. The 16 feet 4 inches wheelbase and many of the panels and later the entire roof on these 30-ft-long single-deckers were made of moulded glass fibre. 4654 to 4721 were modified by being built with an S15-style rear end, which included a repositioned number plate below the central emergency door. 4673's body was completely panelled in glass fibre while the last S14 to be constructed, 4721, had a one-piece roof and front and rear domes. 4590 was also a one-off, being fitted with a full-length translucent roof. Another experiment involved 4671, which was rebuilt with a large illuminated advertisement on both sides of the body at cantrail level that extended from the second bay to halfway along the sixth bay. The new S14s had squared-off mudguards while 4313 and 4700 had at least six S15-style hopper saloon ventilators rather than twelve sliding windows, while 4326 had a mixture of mainly hopper ventilators. Another oddity was 4716, which from new until 1963 was fitted with all-round rubber suspension.

Four of the first batch, 4309/11/23-24 plus 4580, were the only ones fitted with twin rear wheels. Only 4279/79/4332-33/46/48/50-52/4554 and 4567 were originally fitted with the Hobbs automatic transmission à la the prototype, while the rest of the buses had the more prosaic standard DB4 constant-mesh gearbox, but these buses reverted to standard in 1960. All production S14s were fitted with a transmission handbrake, which were legalised on 2 April 1955, but this resulted in a delay in the introduction into service of many of the first batch of UHA-registered S14s.

The experimental introduction of one-man operation (OMO) became an objective as early as 1951 when large rises in fuel taxation began to make serious inroads into the profitability of many of the more rural routes. This was further exacerbated by a steady reduction in passengers as more people could afford to own cars and the steady spread of the availability of television began to seriously damage ridership. The S14s role in the introduction of Midland Red's OMO began on 1 July 1956 at Hereford Garage, setting in motion a chain of events resulting in a series of internal modifications and reductions in seating capacity of these S14 buses. A by-product was that across the three batches of S14s there were well over thirty variations in seating layout in buses equipped for OMO!

The modification to the buses converted to OMO had an illuminated panel on the front panel between the nearside headlight and sidelight, which stated 'PAY AS YOU ENTER'. At the back of the bus there was a reversing light, while the cab door was altered to allow for a ticket machine and coin tray, though there were variations here as well, with many of the conversions having a partition behind the driver with an entrance in front of the leading offside passenger seat. Initial conversions were to the B40F layout, but later seating capacities could be either B42F or B43F. The S14 conversions also evolved with a platform half-height driver's door replacing the sliding door arrangement at the rear of the driving cab bulkhead, while power-operated Setright ticket machines were installed on the half bulkhead just in front of the new door position. A money tray was mounted on the door, which always seemed designed to spill coins all over the cab floor when little more than a quarter full!

This initial OMO experiment was short-lived and ceased on 1 September 1956 because of the lack of an agreement with the Transport & General Workers Union regarding payment for the extra duties. Hereford Garage resumed OMO working on 13 April 1957 and one-man buses were introduced at Shrewsbury, Evesham, Wellington, Banbury, Malvern and Ludlow garages, working on restricted rural services between 1 June 1957 and 4 October 1958. By this time there were about thirty-four S14s converted for OMO, but from 1958 until May 1960 the Union would not allow any further route conversions. Further negotiations enabled more OMO S14 conversions to be introduced in November 1960 at Nuneaton and Swadlincote garages, while in the following twelve months Kidderminster and Tamworth joined the 'OMO Club'. The five garages that had conversions two years earlier also had increased numbers of one-man services, but it must be remembered that each garage only had 'penny numbers' of converted S14s, though by the end of 1962 there were around 100 such buses in operation on mainly rural areas; by the middle of 1964, 'one-manning' was occurring at seventeen Midland Red garages.

The table below shows how a once-simple B44F layout for the S14s was influenced and altered due to the introduction of OMO, but there were also numerous other conversions.

The S14 was, mechanically, an amazingly advanced bus; perhaps only the ill-fated Guy 'Wulfrunian' of 1958 had as many revolutionary features introduced in one go as the S14. As with the Wulfrunian, while they were attractive-looking buses even with the weird single rear tyres, the S14, although the workhorse of the fleet and mechanically reliable, were not something even the most misty-eyed Midland Red employee nor enthusiast could wax lyrical about!

In an attempt to cut down manufacturing and running costs, Midland Red got an amazing single-decker, but at a price. For the passenger, however, the S14 was quite a ghastly bus to ride on. Paring the production S14s weight down to 5 tons 5 cwt resulted in a lack of sound deadening and insulation materials, as well as thin, uncomfortable moquette seat squabs and cushions. The buses also gave a bouncy ride, with frequently rattling and vibrating body panels. Design deficiencies in the buses were common, with heaters being inefficient, and in winter it was common for drivers to stuff rags around the brake, clutch and accelerator pedals to keep out the draughts and to wear extra socks to keep out the cold. The driver's cab was cramped, leading to drivers having to sit uncomfortably, with the throttle pedal seemingly always just out of comfortable reach. The epithet 'boneshakers' could be a justifiable one for these ultra-lightweight S14s.

Year	B40F Built	B40F Converted	B42F Converted	B43F Converted	B44F Built
1955					Nos 4254–4328
1956	Nos 4349/4559–65	No. 4282/4			Nos 4329–48/50–2/4–8/66–89/91–5
1957	No. 4666				Nos 4553/96–4600/51–65/67–75
1958	Nos 4680–90/4703–10/4–5				Nos 4676–79/91–4702/11–3
1959	Nos 4718–21	Nos 4292/4311/4558/68/97–8			
1961			Nos 4272/86/95/4345/4572/98	Nos 4570/6/80/3–4/6–8/90–2/9/4651/6–9/62–3/7/9–70/2/91–2/4–6/9–4702/11–3/7	
1962			Nos 4555–7/66–7/9/77–8/82/4668/77–9/93		

To some extent, the same policy was followed into the 36-ft-long era of the S16 and S17s between 1962 and 1966.

The production buses, according to their capacity and conversion style to OMO, weighed between 5 tons 4 cwt and about 5 tons 16 cwt, though the average weight was between 5¼ and 5½ tons. The first of the S14s to be withdrawn was in April 1967 and the deed was completed in early 1971 when the final twenty-nine were taken off the road. 4255, (UHA 255), the second example of the type, is the sole surviving S14 in preservation.

S15

If the S14 were the 'skin and bone' stage carriage single-deckers, their dual-purpose 'cousins' were an altogether different proposition. Fifty S15s entered service in 1957 with fleet numbers 4601–4650, (601–650 AHA). These were the direct descendent of the heavyweight S13 dual-purpose single-deckers that were augmented instead of replacing the earlier buses. The buses were fitted with higher-ratio back axles and twin sets of rear tyres in order to carry the heavier bodywork, but still retained the standard horizontal BMMO 8.028-litre and four-speed constant-mesh gearbox.

The most obvious difference between the S14 and the S15 was that the standard coach livery of red with a black roof was adopted on the S15, with the two colours being separated by a polished aluminium moulding below the saloon windows, with two short styling strips immediately behind the electrically operated entrance door

on the nearside linking the deep driver's-side cab window with the higher saloon
windows. There was also a thin polished strip on the guttering above the saloon
windows. At the front, the windscreen and the driver's signalling window were deeper,
which gave a much neater and somehow more purposeful look when compared to the
S14 bus body, although it also had the same neatly shaped, half-sized, vertical-barred
radiator grill. The bodywork was largely made of glass fibre, including the front and
rear domes.

The dual-purpose vehicles had basically the same body shell but had a capacity
for forty passengers (DP40F), who would be seated in comfortable Dunlopillo
bucket seats with cheerful and bright fabric cushions and backrests. The interior
colour scheme was a white or yellow ceiling, with buff window panels and the
awful, bilious peony red on the previous S14s and the BMMO D7 double-deckers;
on the S15s, this was mercifully kept to just the panels below the saloon waist
rail. Each of the six side windows was fitted with pull-in hopper ventilators, but
surprisingly the saloon was illuminated by exposed light bulbs. The saloon had,
like all post-war S type underfloor-engined single-deckers, a full-length parcels
rack above the side windows at cantrail level that was divided at the body pillars
to produce a secure luggage space. There was also a small luggage compartment
through a hinged door on the nearside behind the rear axle. This first S15, 4601,
(601 AHA), acted as the class prototype with ordinary pull-in saloon ventilators
and a number of other detailed differences. The well-appointed S15s had an unladen
weight of 5 tons 18 cwt 3 qtrs.

In 1957, the BET Group invited Midland Red to demonstrate their S15s to various
operators. The standard underfloor-engined BET single-deckers at the time were AEC
'Reliances' and Leyland Tiger Cub PSUC1s. As the nationalised BTC Group's successful
Bristol LS and MW underfloor-engined single-deckers were unavailable, the S15 might
have been an alternative to the BET's existing options. Five S15s were demonstrated,
with 4644 going to South Wales, 4645 to Northern General and 4646 was tried out
by Maidstone & District. Potteries Motor Traction ran 4648, while Western Welsh
operated 4649. Manufacturing capacity at Carlyle Road subsequently put paid to any
BET orders.

It was something of a surprise when in 1962, just as the first 36-ft-long S16s were
being planned, Midland Red constructed their final 30-ft-long by 8-inches-wide
single-deckers, which comprised a second class of forty-eight dual-purpose
S15 vehicles. These were numbered 5045–5092, (5045–5092 HA), and were virtually
the same as their predecessors, although only their roofs were painted black and the
side panels were split at floor level with polished trim enhancing the bodywork but,
more practically, making accident damage to the lower panels easier to repair. The
previously exposed radiator filler cap was now covered with a hinged flap.

The S15s were allocated in substantial numbers to Midland Red garages at Digbeth,
Leamington, Lichfield, Nuneaton, Oldbury, Redditch and Worcester, though small
numbers turned up at other garages in Midland Red's operating area. In 1965 the first
fifty vehicles were downgraded to service buses and were repainted into the standard
all-over red livery and equipped for one-man operation, though the vehicles retained

their dual-purpose seats. In 1969 the second batch were similarly downgraded but some received S14 bus seats.

Withdrawals of the first batch began in 1967, with 4624 being taken out of service. This was not the first S15 to be withdrawn, however, as in 1963 4617 was scrapped after catching fire and becoming a total loss. By 1971, the entire 1957 batch had been retired. Withdrawals of the 1962 vehicles took place very rapidly, beginning in 1972 and being completed with just two exceptions during the following year. Two of the second batch, 5056 and 5073, are preserved.

Thus ended Midland Red's last short-length post-war underfloor-engined S type buses. Generally, the S13s were heavy, comfortable and quite long-lived; the S14 were a masterpiece of lightweight construction, but were not desperately popular despite being found operating across the whole of Midland Red territory. The S15 was an excellent dual-purpose vehicle that gave a comfortable ride on limited-stop services and was an able substitute for a coach on a summer's day excursion.

3977, OHA 977
Parked in Central Works, Carlyle Road, is 3977, (OHA 977). The experimental BMMO LA with a Carlyle B44F body, new in April 1952, had more than a passing resemblance to products manufactured by Saunders-Roe. Its service life was quite short, as it had been tested almost to destruction when new. From new it had run with a BMMO 10.5-litre engine, then from 1952 with a Leyland 0.350 5.76-litre engine and from 1957 until its withdrawal in 1961 a standard BMMO 8.028-litre unit. (P. Edgington)

OTC 738

Cradley Heath Garage also had major workshop facilities and because of this it was used as the garage to test buses that were either prototypes or that had experimental features. Midland Red rarely had demonstrator buses from outside manufacturers but the prototype Leyland Tiger Cub PSUC1/13 with a Saunders-Roe B44F body, OTC 738, built in June 1952 was an exception. It was demonstrated within its first year of entering service, not surprisingly, from Cradley Heath Garage, and is passing the Birmingham Museum & Art Gallery entrance in Congreve Street when operating on the 137 route from Gornal Wood, via Brierley Hill, Cradley Heath and on to Halesowen. (S. E. Letts)

4178, THA 778

The prototype BMMO S14 was quite the remarkable bus, with it having so many new features that in its way it was as revolutionary as the REC vehicles of 1935. 4178, (THA 778), was a chassisless construction single-decker bus completed in July 1953 with a 17 foot 6 inch wheelbase and independent front suspension. It had a fully automatic Hobbs Phase 3 gearbox, disc brakes and single rear tyres. In July 1954, it was fitted with a standard David Brown four-speed manual gearbox. After five months of road tests it went into service in December 1954. It is parked in Bearwood bus station when about to leave on the 213 route to the New Inns on Holyhead Road, Handsworth and still has its original horizontally slatted radiator grill. (G. Davies)

4178, THA 778

After 1959, having lost many of its experimental features, 4178, (THA 778), was transferred to the more rural delights of routes operated from Wellington Garage. It is working on the 921 route from Wellington to Little Dawley. At first glance, with a standard radiator grill, 4178 looked like a regular S14, but was always recognisable by its long 17 foot 6 inch wheelbase. The frontal appearance of the S14 was a tidied-up version derived from the previous S13 class, though the windscreen lacked an opening section for the first time. (R. F. Mack)

4255, UHA 255

4255, (UHA 255), was the second bus in the first production batch of ninety-eight lightweight, chassis-less single-deck S14 buses, built with a Carlyle B44F body built on metal section framework. They had independent front suspension and were fitted with a four-speed constant-mesh manual David Brown gearbox coupled to a BMMO 8.028-litre horizontal engine and built with a shortened 16 foot 4 inch wheelbase. The bus is parked alongside the concrete shelters in Worcester bus station before resuming its duty on the 387 service to Evesham via Pershore. It was sold for preservation after its withdrawal in December 1970. (A. Porter)

4271, UHA 271

The Wolverhampton to Ironbridge B92 route was operated by single-deckers due to height restrictions. By the late 1965, S14 single-deckers were being used. 4271, (UHA 271), enters Ironbridge, which at this time had its own version of 'Woolleys'. The village grew because Abraham Darby III built the world's first iron bridge in 1779, which crosses the River Severn with a span of 100 feet. The town is, therefore, a delightful mixture of late Georgian, Regency and Victorian buildings, each marking distinct periods of growth. This was the centre of Telford's 'Cradle of the Industrial Revolution' and the whole area is now a World Heritage Site. (D. R. Harvey Collection)

4303, UHA 303

Single-decker BMMO S14 4303, (UHA 303), new in October 1955, lies-over in Cleveland Street, Wolverhampton, on 21 May 1961. It is standing beneath the Wolverhampton Corporation trolleybus wires and just beyond is the brick and yellow terracotta-faced Central Library, which dated from 1902. The Carlyle B44F-bodied bus is working on the 893 route to Shrewsbury via Ironbridge, where it was briefly allocated to Wellington Garage for six months from January 1961. (G. Pattison)

4309, UHA 309

4309, (UHA 309), was one of the few S14 single-deckers to be equipped with a pair of twin rear wheels, which at once made them look more purposeful and less like Parisian buses, which always had single rear tyres. It is seen in Fairfax Street, Coventry, having just left Pool Meadow bus station. To the left, behind the Ford Zephyr 4 taxi, is the mock-Tudor-fronted Pool Meadow Café, who used an unknown brand of baked bean that adulterated any meal! Behind the S14 is Coventry Transport's 327, (327 CRW), one of the last Metro-Cammell-bodied Daimler CVG6s to be delivered to the municipality. (D. R. Harvey Collection)

4326, UHA 326

While there were only 219 S14s built, there were over thirty variations with seating capacities varying from anything between forty and forty-four seats, which were either equipped for one-man operation or not. A small number of the first batch was delivered with S15-style hopper saloon ventilators. Most of the windows of 4326, (UHA 326), are of this type, although the rear pair of side windows are of the normal sliding type. The bus is parked in Malvern Garage yard. (A. B. Cross)

4558, 558 AHA

On a miserable-looking day, a Carlyle B44F-bodied BMMO S14 is parked in Nuneaton bus station. In the windscreen is a triangular notice used during the first years of one-man operation before illuminated signs were fitted above the nearside headlight. It had been re-seated to a B40F layout in February 1959 before being allocated to Nuneaton Garage for the next six years from May 1959. (J. G. Carroll)

4572, 572 AHA

Stratford-upon-Avon had been, for many years, the focus of Midland Reds more southerly routes. Buses from the more marginal parts of the company's operating area were to be seen in the Red Lion bus station at Bridge Foot. 4572, (572 AHA), new in August 1956, was an S14 that was re-seated to B43F layout for one-man operation in May 1961 and allocated to Banbury Garage. This garage was particularly associated with the S14 class, which were well suited to the rural nature of its operating area. It is fitted with an illuminated OMO sign, having worked on the 480 route from Banbury via Shipston-on-Stour. (P. Redmond)

4583, 583 AHA
The perpendicular, Gothic west tower of St Gregory's Parish Church, built of the local red sandstone, stands on the crest of the low hill above the small village of Offchurch, Warwickshire. On 11 March 1961, 4583, (583 AHA), a Carlyle BMMO S14 new in November 1956, passes beneath the trees in Village Street as it leaves Offchurch, working on the rural X57 service to Leamington, some 3 miles away. (C. W. Routh)

4599, 599 AHA
A rather tired-looking 4599, (599 AHA), travels along Burleys Way in Leicester, where it is seen passing St Margaret's bus station. This BMMO S14 entered service in February 1957 from Sandacre Street Garage and was re-seated in December 1961 to B43F layout for one-man operation. The bus is empty and is not displaying any destinations, suggesting that it is running light back to its home garage. It was withdrawn in January 1969 from Swadlincote Garage. (T. Walker)

4601, 601 AHA

Mechanically, the BMMO S15 was the same as the BMMO S14, with the exception of twin wheels being fitted to the rear axle. The Carlyle DP40F bodywork basic 30-foot metal section framework was finished with very comfortable 'bucket' seats, a brighter interior colour scheme, wider parcel racks and improved heating. Externally, they had a deeper front windscreen than the S14 bus, and added aluminium brightwork. Entering service in April 1957, 4601, (601 AHA), the first S15, leaves London's Victoria coach station. This dual-purpose single-decker had a number of unique features, including hopper saloon windows, an offside, square rear number plate and was the only S15 fitted with a rear luggage boot door. (D. F. Parker)

4622, 622 AHA

How the mighty have fallen! Parked in St Margaret's bus station in Leicester is BMMO S15 622 AHA, where it is identified for its private hire passengers as bus 4. It had entered service in April 1957 from Sandacre Garage in dual-purpose livery and was converted for one-man operation in September 1965. It was downgraded to predominantly bus work, although it managed to retain its original seats and aluminium body brightwork despite being repainted in all-over red bus livery, which made the bus look cheap and unloved. (A. D. Broughall)

4624, 624 AHA

4624, (624 AHA), is in Dudley Street on its way to Digbeth coach station and is passing the premises of George Lewis, who were wholesale stationers. The S15s were well suited to working on the long X96 route linking Shrewsbury, Wellington, Wolverhampton and Birmingham, before travelling eastward to Coventry, Rugby and Northampton. A one-way trip took five hours and twenty-five minutes. There were three round trips westward on the X96 service, while the two eastbound trips were sandwiched between a morning journey from Birmingham to Northampton and a night service from Shrewsbury to Birmingham, so that the Digbeth bus could return to its own garage at the end of the day. (V. France)

4645, 645 AHA

In 1957, BMMO S15s were demonstrated to various BET operators. Five S15s were sent out around the country and seem to have been well received, but for Midland Red's lack of manufacturing capacity, they briefly seemed to be a possible alternative to the contemporary BET orders. 4645, (645 AHA), went on hire to Northern General from October 1957 to April 1958, echoing pre-war orders from this operator for SOS buses up to 1935. The attractive lines of the Carlyle dual-purpose forty-seat body compared well with the products of 'mainstream' coachbuilders and was well finished, despite weighing only 5 tons 18 cwt 3 qtrs. It is operating through Grindon in Sunderland when operating on the 15 route to Consett. (R. F. Mack)

4651, 651 AHA

Travelling into Banbury on the 486 service from Chipping Norton is the first of the final batch of S14 single-deckers. Only the first two of this 1957 class of seventy buses carried reverse AHA registration marks. 4651, (651 AHA), entered service in February 1957 and by 1961 it had been moved from Worcester to Banbury Garage and converted to B43F layout for one-man operation. The bus is being followed by a Bedford S type 5-ton tipper, while on the left is a Hillman Minx Series III saloon. (A. B. Cross)

4671, 671 BHA

4671, (671 BHA), was the most recognisable of all the S14s. It had a pair of incongruously large illuminated advertisement panels attached to the cove panels on both sides, which made this bus look as if it had a pair of stunted wings, like Disney's Dumbo in full flight. When lit up at night, it looked like an illuminated Blackpool tramcar, such was the brightness of the fluorescent panel carrying the advertisement 'M&B Its Marvellous Beer'. It is climbing up the steep hill in Digbeth as it approaches the terminus in front of St Martin's Parish Church in the Bull Ring. (D. R. Harvey Collection)

4673, 673 BHA

4673, (673 BHA), turns into Broad Street from Easy Row opposite the Hall of Memory and the Civic Centre, in a part of Birmingham city centre that would be shortly demolished and replaced by Suffolk Street Queensway and Inner Ring Road tunnel. The bus is working on the 190 service to Kinver on 26 May 1962. This S14 entered service in July 1958 and when seen was yet to be converted to one-man operation. (PhotoFives)

4700, 700 BHA

Parked in Barker Street bus station, Shrewsbury, is BMMO S14 4700, (700 BHA). This was a Shrewsbury bus for eight years from September 1961. This was one of the few S14s fitted with pull-in ventilators in the saloon window bays. When it was equipped for OMO in September 1961, it had illuminated PAYE signs and was down-seated to a B43F layout – the missing seat being replaced by a small luggage rack. (J. G. Carroll)

4708, 708 BHA

If the BMMO S14 was to be found in its natural setting, this was it! 4708, (708 BHA), is in the High Street of the Cotswold town of Chipping Campden with its mellow ochre-coloured Oolitic Jurassic limestone. 4708 is passing the Noel Arms Hotel where Charles II rested after his Scottish army was defeated by the Cromwellians at the Battle of Worcester. The bus is about to return on the 398 Shipston-on-Stour service to Evesham. The 398 route only operated one journey to Evesham on a Saturday afternoon and one on a Sunday at 4.25 p.m. (R. F. Mack)

4721, 721 BHA

The last S14 to be constructed was 4721, (721 BHA). Although another S14 was begun, it was converted to become the prototype BMMO C5 coach, 4722, (722 BHA), in 1958. 4721 entered service in May 1959 already equipped for one-man operation with a B40F layout. It was allocated to Hereford Garage, where it spent its whole life until it was withdrawn in April 1970. It is travelling along High Street on the 429 route and is passing an early 1963 short-wheelbase Land Rover. (D. R. Harvey Collection)

5050, 5050 HA

The X12 limited stop service took two and a half hours to travel from Birmingham via Lichfield and Burton before arriving in the Art Deco-styled Derby bus station. 5050, (5050 HA), dating from July 1962, was one of the second batch of forty-eight dual-purpose vehicles. The S15s were built to a very attractive and successful dual-purpose design, which filled the gap between the BMMO S13 and the BMMO S21 types. They were the last 30-foot-long single-decker type to enter service with Midland Red. The original bucket seats were very comfortable for long-distance services. Unlike the earlier examples, the black of the roof did not extend down the front window pillars to the waist line. (A. D. Broughall)

5061, 5061 HA

The second batch of S15s differed from the 1957 batch by having the side panels split in two with a polished body strip, as well as having a cover for the radiator filler cap. All the S15s used the BMMO KL 8.028-litre engine and in a vehicle weighing 5 tons 18 cwt 3 qtrs, this well-tried engine coupled with different differential ratios enabled the buses to be used on excursion, as well as stage carriage work. 5061, (5061 HA), entered service in September 1962, and within a year it was transferred to Redditch Garage, on whose 142 route it is seen working. It is speeding out of Northfield in Birmingham and is passing the huge mock-Tudor Black Horse public house, which was built in 1929. (R. H. G. Simpson)

5081, 5081 HA

Crossing Dartmouth Square in High Street, West Bromwich, at the junction with Spon Lane, is 5081, (5081 HA). This Carlyle DP40F-bodied BMMO S15 is working on the 252 service and only has to carry on for another 2 miles before terminating at the Farley Clock Tower at Carter's Green. This was a joint service with West Bromwich Corporation and took less than twenty minutes to go from Cape Hill via The Blue Gates public house in Smethwick to Carter's Green, with a fifteen-minute headway. 5081 entered service in December 1962 and operated from Bearwood Garage when working on this service on 7 October 1965. It was withdrawn in July 1972. (A. J. Douglas)

Single-Deckers Taken Over from Leicestershire Independents

Kemp & Shaw

Kemp & Shaw of Mountsorrel ran its first bus services soon after the end of the First World War and although taken over by Allen's Motor Services in 1928, continued to work two main stage carriage service between Leicester via Loughborough and Kegworth to Derby and from Leicester to Birstall and on to Loughborough. The business, along with Allen's Motor Services, was sold to Midland Red on 30 July 1955 and was operated as a subsidiary until it was totally absorbed on 1 January 1959.

(28-29) 4842–43, FJF 89–90

This pair of Guy Arab IIIs with Gardner 5LW engines was delivered in April 1949. They were fitted with Barnard B35F bodies. Barnard bodies were built in Norwich and bus body construction started after the end of the Second World War. In the three years between 1948 and 1950, Barnard made a total of 115 bus and coach bodies, including thirty-seven Guy Arab III double-deckers. Both 4842 and 4843 were withdrawn in 1962.

Single–Deckers Taken Over from Boyer, Rothley

Boyer & Son of Rothley were formed in 1911 and were reputedly the oldest bus company still operating in the county. They operated on the Leicester–Rothley–Mountsorrel–Loughborough corridor along the A6. The company was taken over by Midland Red on 1 January 1959.

4846, HAW 578

4846 was built in June 1951 as one of four integral-construction Sentinel STC6/44 demonstrators that were registered in Shropshire. The somewhat austere 30-ft-long Sentinel B44F body was based on a Beadle design. 4846, (HAW 578), remained in service until 1963.

4847, GUT 543

Bought new in June 1951, GUT 543 was a second Sentinel STC6 and was fitted with the 6SRH2 indirect injection 9.12-litre horizontal engine. It had a Sentinel B44F body and was withdrawn in 1961 as Midland Red 4847.

4848, HJU 546

This was a Leyland Royal Tiger PSU1/9 with a Leyland B44F body that was new in June 1952. It was originally owned by Allen of Mountsorrel as their fleet number 46. HJU 546 was 30 feet long and 8 feet wide and had a Leyland o.600 9.8-litre engine coupled to a synchromesh gearbox and vacuum brakes. It was withdrawn in March 1966 and was sold on to Stevenson of Uttoxeter, where it survived until November 1973.

4843, FJF 90

Above: BMMO took over a pair of Guy Arab IIIs with Gardner 5LW engines that were new in April 1949 from Kemp & Shaw Ltd, Leicester, on 1 January 1959. They had been 28 and 29 in the Kemp & Shaw fleet and, unusually, had Barnard B35F bodies. Barnard was based in Norwich and mainly bodied Guy single- and double-deckers and Austin CXB coaches. Renovated after the takeover by Midland Red, they were transferred to Ludlow Garage after six months, where they both occasionally worked on the tortuous 192 service to Birmingham by way of Clee Hill. 4843, (FJF 90), is seen in St Margaret's bus station in February 1959 when briefly operated by Sandacre Street Garage. It was withdrawn in March 1963. (A. D. Broughall)

4847, GUT 543

Opposite below: In June 1951, Boyer bought a new Sentinel STC6/44 with a Sentinel B44F, which was similar to HAW 578. This was GUT 543 and these monocoque vehicles had a bodywork design that was of somewhat utilitarian appearance. After being taken over on 1 February 1959 and becoming 4847, it was operated by Midland Red from Sandacre Garage. 4847 was withdrawn June 1961. (D. R. Harvey Collection)

4846, HAW 578

HAW 578 had been a demonstrator for the Shrewsbury-based Sentinel Company. It was a STC6/44 model and was fitted with a Sentinel B44F body that was developed from a Beadle design. Built in June 1951, it was sold to Boyer, Rothley, in April 1953. This Sentinel model had a Sentinel 9.12-litre engine with a four-speed constant-mesh gearbox. Boyer was taken over by BMMO on 1 February 1959 and this bus became 4846 in the Midland Red fleet. It was fitted with a BMMO 8.028-litre horizontal engine and rarely ventured away from its former haunts and it is seen here parked in St Margaret's bus station in Leicester. 4846 was withdrawn in June 1963. (A. D. Broughall)

4848, HJU 546

In April 1962, 4848, (HJU 546), turns into Gravel Street from St Margaret's bus station as it
makes its way back to Sandacre Street. This Leyland Royal Tiger PSU1/9 had a Leyland B44F
body and was new in May 1952 to Allen, Mountsorrel. It was bought by Boyer of Rothley
in 1956 and was taken into Midland Red stock as 4848 on 1 February 1959. It was a regular
performer on services towards Loughborough until March 1966. Even then it had a long afterlife,
being sold to Stevenson's of Spath in April 1966, and it stayed in service until withdrawn in
November 1973. (D. R. Harvey Collection)

Early 36-Foot Single-Deckers

S16, 17, 19, 21A

The introduction of the new legal Construction and Use maximum dimensions in 1961 of 36 foot by 8 foot 2½ inches was already anticipated by Midland Red. As a result, Midland Red introduced a lengthened version of the lightweight S14 in 1962, which enabled the company to place into service some of the first 'box' dimension single-deckers in the UK. The development of the new 36-ft-long buses were the first in a long line of the final designs of Midland Red-built single-deckers that were constructed between 1962 and 1970.

The earlier 36-ft-long vehicles were classified S16, S17, S19 and S21A by the company. Their body design could be still be related back to the S9 Mk 1 and all of the first 36-ft-long single-deckers were easily recognisable by their retention of the central emergency rear door and three windows at the rear of the bus – a feature first seen on Midland Red's first SOS 'S' types of 1923, which, by the end of production of the first style of a longer Carlyle body coupled with small multiple-windowed saloon bays by 1966, was beginning to look very dated. The impression was made that little more than fitting in an extra body bay to the existing S14 body had been done on the drawing boards at Carlyle Road. It is somewhat disappointing just how uninspired the appearance of these early 36-ft-long single-deckers actually were!

S16

In February 1961, one of the earliest proposals for a 36-ft-long single-decker was based on the underfloor layout of the experimental underfloor-engined D10 double-decker. Its horizontal engine was to be mounted with the cylinder heads on the inside of the bus, thus allowing for the crankcase to be on the nearside of the vehicle where the ground clearance was not covered by legal restrictions. The arrangement was to have been concluded at the back axle, where a D9/10 offset final drive and similarly offset differential would have kept both the overall height of the bus and the floor line to a minimum. The bus would have seated fifty passengers with a pair of three seats mounted sideways over the rear wheel arches, but crucially the floor line would have been much lower, with just two steps into the saloon. This design for a longer single-decker was some six months in advance of the implementation of the new longer Construction and Use Regulations.

The design staff at Carlyle Road – just for once – bit the bullet and went back to the basic layout of the 30-ft-long S14. In 1954 the S14 prototype was, mechanically, about as advanced as any British single-decker could be, leaving the contemporary AEC Reliance and Leyland Tiger Cub behind. But what was advanced in 1954 was itself being left behind by 1962 and the performance of the new S16s must have been something of a disappointment when compared to the contemporary deliveries of the 100 powerful Leyland Leopard PSU3/4Rs, with bodies supplied by Weymann or Willowbrook between December 1962 and August 1963 to augment the production of buses at Carlyle Road Works. Midland Red had instituted a programme for 600 new saloons to be put on the road between 1962 and 1966, which left Carlyle Road's construction performance unable to keep up with these demands.

The new BMMO bus was designated S16 and had an 18-foot 6-inch wheelbase, while the integral construction bodywork was stretched by one bay to a seven-bay saloon layout. The new bus, designated the S16, had an S15-style front end with the destination number box mounted on the nearside rather than on the offside as per the S14s. As with the last S15s, the lower skirt side and rear panels were separated from the main body panels by a polished aluminium strip so that lower panel damage could be repaired easily. This was a factor with buses with long wheelbases as drivers turning too tightly, particularly on left-hand turns, could easily go over kerbs or foul pavement furniture, resulting in dents.

The first S16 was 5095, (5095HA), which entered service in April 1962 from Cradley Heath Garage. Mechanically, the S16 was virtually the same as the S14, with the standard BMMO KL 8.028-litre horizontal engine being coupled with the standard four-speed constant-mesh David Brown-designed gearbox. By 1962, a constant-mesh gearbox was beginning to be something of an anachronism, except with a minority of operators. The manual gearbox might be fine for a Midland Red driver who had forty years' experience under his belt and who could easily change gear without recourse to the clutch, but the S16s were not so good for the increasing number of employees who were driving buses for the payslip at the end of the month rather than enjoying the challenge of using a clutch and gearbox in perfect harmony. The new design had rubber suspension and disc brakes on both axles. These all-round disc brakes on all the S16s frequently caused problems and so a programme to replace the rear brakes with drums was instigated within a couple of years.

The S16s weighed in at 6 tons 4½ cwt and seated fifty-two passengers. After the successful trials with, 5095, the prototype, the rest of the first batch entered service in December 1962, with the final deliveries arriving by June 1963.

The first class of S16s were numbered 5095–5144, (5095–5144 HA). Initially, about a third of these were delivered to operate on Worcester town services. With their small engines and manual gearboxes, they were patently an underpowered bus, which, despite their increased carrying capacity, rapidly became unpopular with drivers and passengers alike. Their long, lightweight body construction with a high floor line and tightly packed rows of fairly uncomfortable seating that were a lightweight version of those fitted into the recently introduced D9 double-decker, did nothing for passenger comfort. Additionally, they were the last single-deckers to have exposed tungsten-bulb lighting, giving them an interior at night that was akin to sitting in a dimly illuminated tunnel. The only real improvement that the S16s had was a longer overhang in front of the front axle, which enabled the width of the front entrance to be increased to 3 feet 2½ inches and thus improved passenger flow in and out of the bus. The bodies on 5096–5130 were completed by Plaxton, while the remainder of the first batch and the entirety of the second batch were built at Carlyle Road Works.

It was somewhat surprising that after the introduction of the more powerful and driver-friendly S17s in 1963, more S16s were pushed into service. In 1963, 5094, (5094 HA), entered service and was fitted with the later S17-style body, which had flat wheel arches rather than the S16s, which had raised mudguards. This bus and the S19 5093 took over the fleet numbers of the proposed last pair of the second batch of S15s, which were subsequently cancelled. Somewhat surprisingly, another thirty-four S16s, numbered 5512–5545, (6512–6545 HA), entered service in 1964. These buses were intended to be part of the 100 S17s ordered for delivery in 1964, but were built as S16s with S17 bodies in order to use up the leftover supplies of the small KL engine and manual gearboxes that had become redundant in the Midland Red S type building and development programme.

Bearwood, Cradley Heath, Dudley, Evesham, Hereford, Kidderminster, Sandacre Street, Leicester, Ludlow, Nuneaton, Oldbury, Redditch, Shrewsbury, Stafford, Wellington, both Bilston Street and Dudley Road premises at Wolverhampton and Worcester garages all operated S16s. Withdrawal of the S16s began in 1972 and all had been withdrawn by Midland Red by 1976. Fourteen S16 were transferred to West Midland PTE on 4 December 1973 – seven from the first batch of 1963 and seven from the second batch – and none were repainted in PTE's blue and cream livery, with the exception of 5105, (5105 HA), which was only used in this condition as a training bus based at Dudley Garage. All had gone by 1975, with the exception of 5545, (6545 HA), which has been preserved in the excellent care of BaMMOT at Wythall.

S17

In 1963, in order to improve the disappointing performance of the S16s, a new batch of vehicles was placed in service. Lessons had been learnt by the Midland Red staff and although the next batch of buses looked virtually the same as the S16s, these new vehicles were 'a horse of a different colour'.

The new S17s were fitted with the horizontal version of the large D10 engine while also having the new 18-foot 6-inch wheelbase. This 10.45-litre unit was coupled with a Self-Changing Gears semi-automatic, two-pedal-control gearbox. The all-disc braking system on the S16s was not repeated on the new model and all were equipped with disc brakes on the front axle and drums on the rear. The S17 body was a cleaned-up version of that built for the S16s. The side of the buses were, as usual, split, with separate lower panels for ease of replacement and the moulded mudguards were replaced by shaped wheel arches with chrome edging strips. The earlier buses had an offside emergency window in the middle fourth bay, but this was later moved to the offside bay behind the driver's cab from 1964. The buses had a one-piece fibreglass roof and curved corner panels, as well as curved front and rear dome assemblies. As with the earlier S16s, all of the buses were equipped with full-length luggage racks and at last had fluorescent saloon lighting. The S17s, with their larger engines, weighed a fraction over 6 ½ tons – some 6 cwt more than the S16s.

The resultant single-decker was an extremely competent service bus, making them undoubtedly the most successful of all the 36-ft-long BMMO-built lightweight single-deckers, even if their seven-bay bodywork was looking old fashioned. Nearly all the S17s were converted to OMO. This process began in 1966 and the earliest conversions had their seating capacities reduced to either forty-four or forty-eight. It was soon realised that having a lower number of passengers rattling around in a 36-ft-long single-decker was something of a waste of space, which resulted in the seating capacity of OMO S17s reverting to the original B52F layout.

The first batch of S17s were numbered 5446–5511, (6446–6511 HA). The first two entered service in August 1963 and the last few stragglers, completed by Willowbrook, arrived in May 1964. Another 100 S17 were numbered 5546–5595, (BHA 146–195B), and entered service between August and December 1964, while the rest of the batch, 5596–5645, (BHA 596–645C), arrived between February and April 1965. Finally, 5675–5699, (CHA 675–699C), entered service between July and September 1965, and were followed by 5700–5721, (DHA 700–721C), between September and November 1965. The final batch, 5725–5773, (EHA 725–773D), arrived between January and September 1966.

All 261 of the S17 buses had metal section body frames, which were assembled at Carlyle Road, but due to both a lack of capacity and a decline in the number of skilled bodybuilders, trimmers and electricians, which began to affect the viability of Midland Red's tradition of 'home-made' bus-building policy, only seven – 5446 and 5756–5761 – were completed at Carlyle Road Works. The remainder of the bodies were therefore finished and trimmed by other manufacturers. Thus, 5447–61, 5547–71, 5621–45, 5675–5721, 5725–55 and 5762–73 were finished at Plaxton, whose management took on the work despite considering the quality of the bus body shells being supplied to them to be quite awful! 5462–5511, 5546 and 5572–5620 were all completed by Willowbrook at their Loughborough factory.

There were not too many S17 vehicles extensively modified; 5707 was fitted with a Bristol Siddeley torque convertor for three months from February to June 1966, while 5772 ran from June 1971 until July 1975 with a Leyland o.680 engine. 5561 was damaged by fire in 1969 and received S23-style body parts, while during the following year 5557, (AHA 157B), was more extensively rebuilt after being partly burnt out and was always easily identifiable as it had the S23-style peaked front dome.

The S17s were widely allocated around the Midland Red system to Digbeth, Bromsgrove, Cradley Heath, Evesham, Hereford, Kidderminster, Sandacre Street,

Leicester, Lichfield, Malvern, Nuneaton, Oldbury, Redditch, Rugby, Shrewsbury, Swadlincote, Tamworth, Wolverhampton's Dudley Road and Worcester garages.

Some seventy-nine S17s were transferred to West Midland PTE in December 1973 and of these all but 5705, which was acquired with severe accident damage and therefore never ran for the PTE, were repainted in West Midland livery in November 1973, with 5762, (EHA 762D), being used as a trial repaint in readiness for the takeover. It was perhaps surprising that, in view of the unwillingness of the Midland Red Company to be effectively taken over, many of the Midland Red stock of buses were chosen for repainting, and were repainted in blue and cream at Carlyle Road Works. It was obviously done on a commercial basis but to the outside observer it did seem to be rubbing a good deal of salt into the already writhing Midland Red operation, which was effectively condemned by the heartland being taken out of their operating area by the West Midland PTE takeover on 4 December 1973.

West Midland PTE withdrawals began in 1974, although three S17 managed to remain in service until 1977. The Midland Red withdrawals began in April 1975 when 5484 was withdrawn, while the last six of the class, 5473, 5479–5480, 5490, 5555, 5767, survived into 1979, when they too were taken out of service. Fortunately, 5479, (6479 HA), the last of the class to be withdrawn in November 1979, was preserved, while 5767, (EHA 767D), is part of the BaMMOT collection at Wythall.

LS18

To augment the production of buses at Carlyle Road Works, a total of 100 Leyland Leopard PSU3/4R single-deck buses with BET Federation-style bodies entered service between December 1962 and August 1963. These 36-ft-long Leyland Leopard PSU3/4Rs had an 18 foot 6 inch wheelbase and were fitted with the Leyland o.600 9.8-litre engine and pneumocyclic gearbox. These were classified LS18 by Midland Red and were the first single-deck vehicles purchased by BMMO from an outside manufacturer since the solitary Dennis Lancet 2 in 1938! They were to be the first of 550 vehicles based on the Leyland Leopard chassis that BMMO bought with both bus and coach bodywork. The Leyland Leopard PSU3 became the standard BET single-decker with similarly styled bodies being supplied to the Northern General Group, Trent and other BET group members.

The LS18s must have been a revelation as they were everything the contemporary S16 was not! They were the first new single-deckers in the fleet since 1940 to have separate chassis and bodies, were more powerful, had the free-revving 9.8-litre Leyland o.600 engine coupled to a pneumocyclic semi-automatic gearbox with two-pedal control, were much quicker through the gears, were easier to drive (except for their very heavy steering), had air brakes and their heavyweight bodies did not shake or rattle!

The class of 100 vehicles was numbered 5145–5244, (5145–5244 HA), but this contained five different batches, four different types and two bodybuilders. LS18s numbered 5145–5169 had Weymann B53F bodies and were delivered between

December 1962 and February 1963. 5170–5174 received Willowbrook B53F bodywork and all five arrived in August 1963. The dual-purpose LS18A were the Willowbrook DP48F bodied 5175–5194 and were delivered from Loughborough between April and July 1963. The final fifty, 5195–5244, reverted to Willowbrook B53F bodies and entered service between December 1961 and February 1963.

When new, the buses were painted in an overall red BMMO livery and coded LS18, while the twenty DP48F vehicles were coded LS18A and were painted in the distinguished BMMO coach livery of red with a black roof. The bodywork from both coachbuilders was broadly similar, though the main identifying feature was that the front side lights on the Weymann buses were mounted lower on the front apron. All the LS18s were converted to one-man operation from 1966, while the LS18A were converted to one-man operation from November 1968 and downgraded to bus work as type LS18s with B53F seating from January 1971.

On 3 December 1973, 5148/60-3/73/5/7/95/8/5200-1/12/23/5/32/9/43-4 were taken over by WMPTE and were down-seated to B51F by February 1977. The first WMPTE withdrawals started in 1976 and the last ones went in 1978, while the first normal Midland Red withdrawals began in June 1977 and were completed in June 1980. 5212, (5212 HA), was later sold for preservation.

S19

The solitary S19 was 5093, (5093 HA), which took the fleet number not used when the forty-ninth and the fiftieth S15s were cancelled in favour of 36-ft-long prototypes. 5093 was effectively the first S17 bus to be built as it was fitted with a Self-Changing Gears semi-automatic gearbox instead of the David Brown constant-mesh manual gearbox of the S16s. The bus could also be recognised as a modified S17 as it had an instrument binnacle mounted just below the steering wheel in the style only fitted to the S17s, as well as having a shallower rake to the angle of the steering column when compared to the S16 vehicles. The bus was also different underneath as it was fitted with a modified independent suspension system that consisted of rear axle rubber units on the front, as opposed to all other BMMO saloons that featured separately designed units on the front and rear axles. 5093 HA retained its experimental suspension throughout its working life.

Trials of the S19 commenced with 5093 at Digbeth Garage in July 1964, before the bus was introduced into service later that year, operating from Dudley and later Shrewsbury garages. The S19 was fitted with a modified style of radiator grill, which later became standard on the S22 and S23 buses, as well as having the smooth sided bodywork of the S17s. It remained in service, operating latterly from Worcester Garage from January 1965 until it was withdrawn in April 1975. It was scrapped three months later.

S21A

Three of the S17 body shells built in 1965 were taken out of the normal run of the batch and were completed as dual-purpose prototypes, being classified as S21As.

The three single-deckers were numbered 5722–5724, (DHA 722–724C), and were completed by Plaxton as DP48F vehicles. All three were painted in Midland Red's attractive dual-purpose red livery with black roofs and chrome trim. 5723 had a forced ventilation system and was the only one of the trio to have air induction scoops, which drew air into the saloon, passing air into slots in the luggage racks. Rather more unusually, this dual-purpose bus also had saloon ventilators. In order to gauge passenger reaction, all three had different interior trims. 5722's interior was coloured in grey, fawn and red trim and 5723's saloon was trimmed in a multi-coloured black, fawn, grey and primrose, while the last of the triumvirate, 5724, was trimmed in a simpler blue and grey scheme. It was this last combination that was chosen for the later dual-purpose S22 vehicles, presumably as the others were a little sickening to the eye!

When new, the three S21As were allocated, in order, to Hereford, Lichfield and Southgate Street, Leicester garages and in December 1966 were reclassified as S22. After conversion to OMO in 1970, they were reclassified back to their original intended S17 type in June 1971. The three S21As were further downgraded to almost the point of humiliation when they were all fitted out as B52F service buses, with 5723 being converted in May 1972 while the other two were treated in December 1975. All three buses were withdrawn in 1977.

In many ways, the trio of S21A single-deckers were the prototypes for the later S21 and S22 single-deckers, but although mechanically similar and well finished, they were the last of the multi-windowed breed of 36-ft-long single-deckers. Thus they appeared, externally at least, most unlike the vehicles that followed them, but were nonetheless 'classy', if somewhat old-fashioned-looking PSVs, being a stretched version of the well-liked dual-purpose S15 buses.

This first generation of 36-ft-long integral single-decker buses entered service between 1962 and 1966 and accounted for 250 vehicles. Unfortunately, the first type of box dimension BMMO single-deckers, the S16s, of which there were eighty-five, were not very good, having the small 8.028-litre engine coupled to a manual gearbox and an uncomfortable driving position. They cast a shadow over what came later and, by association, gave the later classes a somewhat undeserved reputation. Like the S17s, S19s and S21As, they were fitted with an unimaginative body design that looked dated when it was first introduced on the S16s in 1962. The 161 S17s, on the other hand, were very successful service buses, having the large BMMO 10.5-litre engine coupled to semi-automatic gearboxes, which was basically the mechanical layout that was continued until the end of BMMO bus production in 1970 with the S23 class. Finally, the S21As pointed the way forward to the last generation of longer dual-purpose buses, despite still using the S16–17 type of multi-windowed body.

Summary of Early 36-Foot-Long BMMO S Type Single-Deckers

Class	Fleet No.	Registration No.	Body details	In service	Withdrawn
S16	Nos 5094–5144 Nos 5512–5545 (85)	5094–5144 HA 6512–6545 HA	5094–95/ 5131–44 Carlyle B52F 5096–5130 Carlyle/Plaxton B52F Carlyle B52F	1962–1963 1964	1972–1976
S17	Nos 5446–5511 Nos 5546–5645 Nos 5675–5721 Nos 5725–5773 (161)	6446–6511 HA AHA 146–195C BHA 596–45C CHA 675–700C DHA 701–721C EHA 725–773D	5446, 5756–5761 Carlyle B52F 5447–61, 5547–71, 5621–45, 5675– 5721, 5725–55 and 5762–73 Carlyle/Plaxton B52F 5462–5511, 5546 and 5572–5620 Carlyle/Willowbrook B52F	1964–1966	1974–1979
S19	No.5093 (1)	5093 HA	Carlyle B52F	1963	1975
S21A	Nos 5722–5224 (3)	DHA 722–724C	Carlyle/Plaxton DP48F	1966	1977

5094, 5094 HA

Above: One of eight BMMO S16s new into service in March 1963, and allocated to Lichfield Garage, 5122, (5122 HA), stands at the temporary bus stop in St Martin's Ringway with the still-unopened new entrance to New Street station behind it. To the right is the soon to disappear Worcester Street and the tall gabled premises, which were very shallow and were really only built to hide the entrance of the railway tunnel. It would all be demolished and replaced by the famous Rotunda Building. 5122 is seen about to leave on the 112 service to Burton. (A. D. Broughall)

5093, 5093 HA

Opposite below: 5093, (5093 HA), entered service in July 1964 as the solitary S19. It was basically a BMMO S17 with a semi-automatic gearbox and a large 10.45-litre BMMO engine, but it had an experimental rubber suspension system, which it retained throughout its life. Parked in Worcester bus station, 5093 is about to work on the 420 service to Hereford via Bromyard, and by now it has been fitted with a front grill from a BMMO S22. It was finally withdrawn from Padmore Street Garage, Worcester, in April 1975. (D. R. Harvey Collection)

5122, 5122 HA

Unusually for Midland Red, the BMMO S16 was not a particularly successful vehicle design. The BMMO KL 8.028-litre engine, with a power output of only 98 bhp, proved underpowered in a 36 foot, fifty-two-seater bus and the David Brown manual crash gearbox was unpopular with drivers who were getting used to the SCG semi-automatic gearbox fitted to the contemporary BMMO D9 double-deckers. Manual gear changes and fare collection made S16s unsuitable for one-man operation and therefore they were mostly used on crew-operated routes. 5122, (5122 HA), works on the 765 service via Atherstone, with the usual waterstain from the radiator discolouring the front grill. (A. D. Broughall)

5136, 5136 HA

Passing the, at the time, recently closed Midland Red Chief Parcels Office in Pershore Street, is the almost new BMMO S16, 5136, (5136 HA). This bus had entered service in April 1963 from Bromsgrove Garage and is being used on the 145 service to Bromsgrove via Cotteridge, West Heath, Rednal and Barnt Green. When the Birmingham and Black Country service of Midland Red were taken over by WMPTE on 3 December 1973, 5136 was at Oldbury Garage and survived with West Midlands until July 1975. The bus has just left the newly opened Bull Ring bus station to the left of the steps that led up to Smallbrook Ringway. (A. D. Broughall)

5148, 5148 HA

A fully laden 5148, (5148 HA), leaves Dudley bus station when working on the 283 service to the unusually named Fatherless Barn municipal housing estate in Cradley. This was a bus classified by Midland Red as their LS18 type and was a Leyland Leopard PSU3/4R. This bus was one of twenty-five numbered between 5145 and 5169 with Weymann B53F bodywork. It entered service in December 1962 from Cradley Heath Garage and was working for Midland Red before it was equipped for OMO in November 1968. It went to WMPTE in December 1973 and survived, having been painted in their livery, until January 1978. (L. Mason)

5169, 5169 HA

Waiting to leave the old Burton bus station on land formerly owned by the railway is 5169, (5169 HA). It is waiting to return to Leicester via Coalville on the 668 route when allocated to Swadlincote Garage. 5169 was the last of the Weymann bus-bodied Leyland Leopard PSU3/4Rs and differed from the larger batch of Willowbrook-bodied examples by having slightly smaller, and lower-mounted, front side lights, with a square rather than rectangular ventilation grill below the illuminated 'MIDLAND' sign. The whole order from Midland Red was for 100 chassis and these had the distinction of being the first single-deckers bought new by the company from a proprietary chassis manufacturer. (R. F. Mack)

5183, 5183 HA

There were just twenty Willowbrook-bodied DP48F dual-purpose Leyland Leopard PSU3/4Rs, numbered 5175–5194, and these were classified as type LS18A. They had black roofs in the style of Midland Red coaches and were initially used on duplicate coach and express services. 5183, (5183 HA), entered service in April 1963 from Digbeth Garage but was, unfortunately, severely damaged in a fire and was withdrawn in early 1968. It is in Mount Street bus station in Nottingham when waiting to leave on the two hour and forty-five minute journey to Birmingham by way of Ashby-de-la Zouch, Tamworth and Sutton Coldfield. (D. R. Harvey Collection)

5212, 5212 HA

Some eighteen Leyland Leopard PSU3/4R LS18s were taken over on 3 December 1973 and were repainted in the standard WMPTE blue and white livery. One of these was 5212, (5212 HA). New in December 1962, it was delivered to Digbeth Garage and was fitted for one-man operation six years later. 5212 is in Hill Street when working on the former BCT 48 tram route. It passed to WMPTE and was operated from both the former Birmingham City Transport garages at Moseley Road and Yardley Wood before being withdrawn in October 1978. After a charmed life of twenty years, it was finally passed to the Transport Museum at Wythall for preservation. (D. R. Harvey Collection)

5237, 5237 HA

On 4 April 1976, Willowbrook B53F-bodied Leyland Leopard PSU3/4R, 5237, (5237 HA), is working on the L43 town service – one of four Leamington Spa town routes to nearby Warwick. The bus, operating beneath some of the Georgian buildings of Leamington, is painted in the NBC Midland Red poppy red livery with a single white strip beneath the saloon windows. It was new in February 1963 and spent its whole life at Leamington Garage until it was withdrawn in April 1979. (A. D. Packer)

5244, 5244 HA

The Leyland Leopard PSU3/4Rs were, compared to the contemporary S16 and S17s, and except for their heavy steering, a delight to drive, but were ideal for inter-urban journeys when their 'long-legged' characteristics could be used in full. 5244, (5244 HA), a Willowbrook B53F-bodied Leyland Leopard PSU3/4R, was fitted with a stylish BMMO badge on the front apron, as were the contemporary DD11 Daimler Fleetline double-deckers. This was strange as the 'indigenous' BMMO single-deckers were never fitted with maker's badges! The bus is turning out of High Street into Whitburn Street in the Upper Town of Bridgnorth in front of Northgate with the aid of a policeman when working on the 971 service to Ludlow. (R. F. Mack)

5462, 6462 HA

In 1963, Midland Red introduced the BMMO S17, which was similar in appearance to the BMMO S16, but had the BMMO 10.5-litre engine and four-speed SCG semi-automatic gearbox. Although being used as a crew-operated bus, this combination of larger engine and gearbox made the S17 a really useful, potential OMO single-decker. 5462, (6462 HA), stands outside its terminus at Hungarton (a village known as the home of Blue Stilton cheese), having arrived on the 10-mile journey from Leicester via Scraptoft. (D. R. Harvey Collection)

5473, 5473 HA

Emerging from the stygian gloom of Birmingham's Bull Ring Centre bus station into Edgbaston Street is 5473, (5473 HA). With Willowbrook-finished bodywork, it was one of forty BMMO S17s numbered 5462–5511. It is seen working on the 147 service to Redditch via Birmingham's Pershore Road and Alvechurch. The bus is wearing the uniformly awful corporate NBC livery of poppy red with a broad white stripe, which quickly looked drab as the colour soon faded. It was one of the last six S17s to remain in service, finally being withdrawn in April 1979. (D. R. Harvey)

5480, 6480 HA

Parked outside the George Hotel in the Market Place, Ashby-de-la-Zouch, is 5480, (6480 HA), which was delivered in January 1964. By this time the moulded, raised wheel arch surrounds had been replaced by a much less fussy-looking thin polished strip. It is working on the 668 service and is on its way from Leicester to Burton. This S17 had a body completed by Willowbrook on Metal Section frames that were fabricated at Central Works before being sent to Loughborough for finishing. It spent its entire life working in the East Midlands, being variously operating from Coalville, Wigston and Nuneaton garages. (R. F. Mack)

5520, 6520 HA

Between January and July 1964 BMMO produced a second batch of thirty-four S16 single-deckers. At the time, Central Works at Carlyle Road was phasing out the BMMO 8.028-litre engines and had too many unused in stock to waste, while also having a number of four-speed manual gearboxes retrieved from early BMMO C5 coaches that had been converted to five-speed gearboxes for motorway use. It is likely that the second batch of S16s were assembled simply to use up parts that had become obsolete with the introduction of more advanced BMMO S17. 5520, (6520 HA), which was new in March 1964 to Sandacre Street Garage, would have a service life of less than twelve years. It is working on the 672 route to Seagrave, Leicestershire on 22 July 1967, and is standing in front of the White Horse public house, with the sixteenth-century All Saints' Parish Church beyond. (D. R. Harvey Collection)

5538, 6538 HA

5538, (6538 HA), negotiates the roadworks in the soon-to-be-demolished Stafford Street in Birmingham during 1964. Straddling the gap of Ryder Street behind the bus is the large premises of Harris & Sheldon, shopfitters, to the left, and the semi half-timbered electrical tool shop of W. H. Price to the right. This BMMO S16 entered service in June 1964 from Swadlincote Garage and is seen coming towards its terminus in Station Street, Birmingham, on the 112 service from Burton-on-Trent via Lichfield, which took one hour and forty minutes. (R. H. G. Simpson)

5563, AHA 163B

On 16 March 1967, a year before it was converted to OMO, 5563, (AHA 163B), a BMMO S17 that was new in September 1964 to Shrewsbury Garage, is working on the local Shrewsbury S13 town service to Copthorne via Woodfield Road. It was one of a batch of twenty-five Plaxton-finished Carlyle B52F buses completed between August and September 1964, with its saloon emergency window being located in the fourth offside bay. 5563 later went to Harts Hill Garage, which was taken over by WMPTE, and it was withdrawn from there in February 1976. (PhotoFives)

5677, CHA 677C

5677, (CHA 677C) is seen parked in Bridgefoot bus station next to the Red Lion public house in Stratford-on-Avon. It is soon to load up with passengers, having arrived from Bromsgrove by way of Redditch, Studley and Alcester on the 339 route. Taking one hour and twenty minutes, this was the type of cross-country Midland Red bus service upon which the company's reputation was founded. This BMMO S17 had a Plaxton-finished Carlyle B52F body and entered service in July 1965, being converted to one-man operation and having illuminated PAYE signs. (D. F. Parker)

5695, CHA 695C

New in September 1965, BMMO S17 5695, (CHA 695C), is operating in the Black Country on the 244 route to Cradley Heath while in its later Midland Red livery. The bus had a Plaxton-finished Carlyle B52F body and was converted to OMO in March 1968. It was allocated to Dudley Garage in May 1971 before being transferred to WMPTE on 3 December 1973. It survived until April 1976. (D. Wilson)

5712, DHA 712C
Parked in Shrewsbury bus station and wearing NBC poppy red and white band livery, 5712, (DHA 712C), has arrived in the county town on the 964 service from Bridgnorth and Much Wenlock. New in October 1965, 5712 was allocated to Shrewsbury Garage for nearly all of its twelve-year life. The B52F bodywork on this BMMO S17 was finished by Plaxton to BMMO design, which still had the antiquated style of the three rear window and central emergency door layout. (J. G. Carroll)

5761, EHA 761D

Above: 5761, (EHA 761D), was the last of a late batch of six S17s that had Carlyle B52F bodywork that was completed in-house at Central Works. The bus complied with the latest legislation by having an emergency window mounted on the offside, behind the driver's cab. Fitted for one-man operation from new, 5761 entered service in September 1966 from Malvern Garage and after five years was transferred to Dudley, from where it was transferred to WMPTE and was painted in their livery of blue and cream but only had a service life of ten years. The bus is parked in the shadow of the tall, gloomy-looking Cavendish House office block in the Fisher Street section of Dudley bus station when about to work on the ten-minute journey on the D17 service to Woodside. (A. J. Douglas)

5723, DHA 723C

Opposite below: There were just three BMMO S21As built and all entered service in January 1966. 5723, (DHA 723C), was the middle of the trio of these forty-eight-seater dual-purpose single-deckers. All had different coloured interiors, with this one having a black, fawn, primrose and grey interior colour scheme. Their standard S17-style bodywork was finished by Plaxton to BMMO design, which was heavily disguised by the new red and black BMMO coach livery, and included the fitting of roof-mounted air scoops as part of the forced ventilation system in the luggage racks. Strangely, even with this, the bus still had sliding saloon ventilators! 5723 is leaving Broadgate bus station in Nuneaton on the very long X91 service, starting in Leicester in the east and crossing the Midlands by way of Coventry, Warwick, Stratford-on-Avon, Evesham, Worcester, Great Malvern to Hereford in the south-west of their operating area. The complete journey took five and a half hours! 5723 was reclassified as an S22 in December 1967 and was converted to one-man operation in June 1970 before being downgraded to an S17 in 1972 with a B52F layout. It ran for another five years before being withdrawn. (Hazeldine)

The Final Midland Red-Built Single-Deckers

S20

5839–5848 (JHA 839–848E)

Coupled with the imminent takeover by the THC, the question about continuing the expensive 'home-made' products of BMMO at Carlyle Road was beginning to have an effect on ordering and manufacturing their own buses. The result was that ten new Leyland Leopard PSU3/4R chassis were ordered in 1966. Given the designation LS20, their arrival was symptomatic in the change of policy that was about to end Midland Red's bus manufacturing.

Ten Leyland Leopard PSU3/4R with Leyland o.600 engines arrived as 5839–5848, (JHA 839–848E). They had Willowbrook DP49F bodywork that incorporated the split BET standard curved windscreen and rear windows with peaked front domes and a single-line combined destination and route number box. They had high-backed seats and forced ventilation and were very attractive vehicles in their red and black livery and blue upholstered high-backed seats. The first five were delivered in March 1967 and the second half arrived during the following month. When new, they were typically allocated in ones and two around Midland Red's garages, with Digbeth getting two (5839 and 5846), and two more going to Southgate Street, Leicester (5842 and 5848). They were all modified to OMO in 1970 and their conversion to B53F began in 1978. Withdrawals began in May 1979 and all were gone by April 1981.

BMMO S21, S22 and S23 Single–Deckers

The S21, S22 and S23 single-deckers were the last vehicles built by Midland Red at Carlyle Road's Central Works. The first SOS buses had been constructed in 1923 and, until about the early 1960s, it looked as if the tradition would continue indefinitely. Alas, changes in work patterns in the West Midlands led to the rapid decline in the skilled engineering and bodybuilding staff, especially when skilled bodybuilders were being attracted by better pay and working conditions elsewhere in the West Midlands motorcar industry. As a result, the cost of building new vehicles began to escalate and it soon became obvious that, economically, continued vehicle production was becoming unviable. When the ambitious requirement of 600 new vehicles was announced in 1962, the first sign of looking elsewhere was when 100 Leyland Leopard single-deckers, as well as another 100 Alexander-bodied Daimler Fleetlines, were ordered. It became gradually obvious that these vehicles were cheaper to purchase than the home-made product and that they were more robust than their Carlyle-built counterparts.

By 1966, Donald Sinclair, the long-serving General Manager and underfloor-engine pioneer, had retired and although he was succeeded by Mr Womar, who had been his long-standing deputy, the driving force and enthusiasm for home-made products was rapidly waning.

However, even as late as September 1967, Midland Red's mechanical designers had prepared detailed drawings of a 36-ft-long vehicle, which was similar to the Bristol RE that had reached the production stage some three years earlier. The BMMO KL 10.5-litre rear-engine was mounted longitudinally behind the Self-Changing Gears semi-automatic gearbox. It appears that although this advanced design was never produced, the company obviously hadn't quite given up on building their own BMMO-built vehicles. The fact that Midland Red designers and engineers had designed a rear-engined single-decker in 1935, after all the S type underfloor-engined buses, it was somewhat ironic that the proposed position of the engine on Midland Red's single-deckers had gone full circle!

The company became a subsidiary of the National Bus Company (NBC) on 1 January 1969, but despite them largely taking the blame for the end of Midland Red's unique tradition of vehicle-building, the real reasons for ceasing vehicle production had been for all to see some years early; all the NBC group did was not authorise the construction of any new buses, as the company was losing money and vehicle-building had to cease for the company to survive.

The Last Hurrah! BMMO S21

The thirty S21s were designed by BMMO for use specifically as a semi-coach vehicle rather than a dual-purpose bus, with higher specifications than a bus and were fitted out with more comfortable seating. They were intended for use on longer-distance stage carriage services during the week and for duplicate coach excursions at weekends and from the outset were intended to be operated by a crew of two. The S21 was the most attractive design of all the BMMO 36-ft-long saloons and were subtly different from the dual-purpose S22 single-deckers.

The mechanical running units on the S21s were almost identical to the BMMO S17, having a BMMO 10.5-litre engine and a Self-Changing Gears semi-automatic four-speed gearbox, although the rear axle differential ratios were originally set higher in order to allow a better motorway top speed. Braking was also the same as the S17, with all-round disc brakes and a transmission handbrake that was far more convenient to operate by the driver as it was operated by a small lever located below the driver's signalling window. The rear disc brakes on the S21s were later converted to drums due to excessive pad wear, as had happened with the S17s. The thirty vehicles were all altered at Carlyle Road Works while some S21s were fitted with drum brakes on the front as well.

Numbered 5849–5878, (JHA 849–868E and LHA 869–878E), the seven-bay look was abandoned as the new 36-ft-long body was of six-bay construction, being based on the thirty BMMO CM6 Motorway coaches. For the first time since the construction of the S15 dual-purpose single-deckers, the bodywork for the S21s was built by

BMMO at Central Works, Carlyle Road, and they were constructed with a one-piece fibreglass roof that was first developed on the earlier S16 and S17. The side windows were fixed and ventilation was by forced air through two roof scoops at the rear that was delivered to each individual passenger by an adjustable rotary nozzle set into the luggage rack. Although the S21s used the windscreen and entrance door of the type fitted to the S17, they had a one-piece rear window and no rear destination number box. When new, the S21s were originally equipped with very small nearside number boxes but slightly larger boxes were later fitted during their first overhaul, although a small number of vehicles were never modified. There was an emergency door, which was set into the rear offside of the bus, and an emergency window on the nearside in the sixth bay. At the rear, the vehicles had a two-door luggage compartment and had a one-piece rear window, eschewing the need, for the first time in many years, to have a central rear emergency door.

Additionally, the S21s had a new style of fibreglass curved front and rear dome. Uniquely, the thirty vehicles were equipped with an attractive front grille with ten horizontal slats that covered the whole of the front apron, with the headlights and single nearside spotlight being incorporated into the design. The vehicles also had polished raised aluminium mouldings under the saloon windows with raised metal scroll coach-style 'Midland Red' fleet names at the front, side and rear. As if to emphasise their role as semi-coaches, the S21s were painted in a modified version of the classic coach livery, with the early examples being delivered in red with a black roof, but vehicles after fleet number 5860 had a maroon roof. Internally, the vehicles were equipped with forty-nine blue vinyl semi-coach seats of the same scheme as 5724 – the last of the S21As. Despite their luxury equipment, these vehicles weighed 7 tons 11 cwt.

The S21s entered service in May 1967, when the first half of the class were put on the road, but it took until November 1967 before the final vehicle, 5878, entered service. The long period of construction rather reflected the production capacity at Central Works that was being experienced by Midland Red at this time.

From 1970, BMMO began to convert the S21s to one-man operation, while at the same time converting some of them into service buses, whose seating variations ranged from B49F, B51F or B53F. These bus seats were taken from early examples of the later BMMO S23s, numbered 5916–5923, as these vehicles had been fitted with non-standard rexine-covered S17-style seats from new. The redundant S21 seats were later fitted to LC9 type Plaxton-bodied Leyland Leopard PSU4/4R coaches 5829 and 5837, while these extra coach seats were used to increase the seating capacity of the rest of the batch of LC9 coaches, 5824–5838, (GHA 324–338D), from C36F to C40F.

The allocation of these thirty S21s was the usual scattergun method, with only Digbeth, Sutton Coldfield, Bearwood and Bromsgrove garages getting two or more. The remaining S21s went to Cradley Heath, Evesham, Kidderminster Nuneaton, Redditch, Rugby, Sandacre Street in Leicester, Wellington, Wigston and Worcester garages. The transfer of 413 Midland Red vehicles to West Midlands PTE on 3 December 1973 saw 5849–53, 5859, 5870 and 5876–77 being acquired by West Midlands and although all but two retained their DP49F layout, 5849 and 5850 had already been converted to B51F. The PTE examples were withdrawn in 1977 and 1978 while those still with Midland Red were taken out of service between May 1979 and June 1980. Although not very long-lived, the attractive-looking S21s were successful in their role as semi-coaches and, unlike the comfortable dual-purpose S22s, they were virtually coaches in a bus-like body shell.

There are three S21 in preservation. 5868, (JHA 868E), is part of the BaMMOT collection at Wythall while 5870, (LHA 870F), is now preserved at the Aldridge Bus Museum. 5878, (LHA 878F), which was originally purchased by staff at Rugby Garage, from where it was finally operated, is now privately owned and is in store.

BMMO S22

The BMMO S22 was designed specifically for one-man operation for use on the many long distance Midland Red stage carriage 'X'-numbered services and private hire work. Mechanically, the BMMO S22 was identical to the BMMO S21, with a BMMO 10.5-litre engine coupled to an SCG semi-automatic four-speed gearbox. The bodywork was also based on the CM6T, with six large fixed side windows and a forced air ventilation system, which pulled in air by way of two rear-mounted air scoops above the rear dome of the saloon. Additionally, the S22s were also equipped with rear luggage compartments, which in later years, when the dual-purpose vehicles were relegated to bus work, were panelled over. The vehicles had a seating capacity of only forty-five, which was perhaps surprising as one might have expected these dual-purpose vehicles to seat at least as many as the S21 semi-coaches. However, with a large luggage pen replacing four seats immediately behind the drivers cab, and being equipped for one-man operation from new, it was a justifiable decision to keep the seating capacity down. The interior differed from the type S21 in that the seats were deep cushioned and high-backed, being covered in red vinyl with no separate head rests, but with a top grab rail.

The thirty-seven S22s were given the fleet numbers 5879–5915, (MHA 879–903F and PHA 904–915G), and all were built and finished at Midland Red's own Central Works at Carlyle Road. The S22s looked different from the previous semi-coaches. The most obvious alteration was the front radiator grill, which was very similar to that of the BMMO D9 double-decker. While this grill looked fine on the double-decker and infinitely better than the S16, S17 and S19 radiator grill, it was something of a disappointment when compared to the handsome chromed front aspect of the S21s. Additionally, the S22s had illuminated 'Pay as you Enter' signs above the nearside headlight and alongside the front entrance doors above the nearside wheel arch was a yellow flip-over 'Limited Stop', but this feature was soon removed due to the frailty of the flip-over cover. 5879–5893 were fitted with the small destination number display boxes while 5894 onwards had larger front destination number displays – though the earlier fifteen were later fitted with the larger type of box when they were overhauled. One of the few oddities of the class was 5903, (MHA 903F), which in addition to having a forced ventilation system also had sliding ventilators in some of the side windows – a combination that had been first seen on the S21As.

Unusually, all the S22 dual-purpose vehicles were delivered in an overall red BMMO bus livery, which was a great pity as they would have been well-suited to the attractive red and black dual-purpose and coach colours. A new style of gold transfer fleet names were placed on the centre panels at the sides, which was unique to the S22s. The unladen weight of these dual-purpose vehicles was fairly consistent at 7 tons 4 cwt.

Deliveries began in January 1968 and were completed by October 1968. Initially, the vehicles were allocated far and wide around the Midland Red garages, with Banbury, Bearwood, Coalville, Cradley Heath, Digbeth in Birmingham, Evesham, Kidderminster, Leamington, both Sandacre Street and Southgate Street in Leicester, Lichfield, Ludlow, Redditch, Shrewsbury, Swadlincote, Tamworth, Wellington, Wigston, Wolverhampton and Worcester all receiving penny numbers of the class. Later transfers went to both Hinckley and Nuneaton garages and, with the exception of 5894, which was an accident victim and was the first withdrawal in May 1977, the Midland Red examples were all withdrawn between December 1979 and September 1980. 5886, 5889, 5899, 5902–3 and 5908–11 were transferred to WMPTE on 3 December 1973 and all were withdrawn between 1976 and 1979. Only two examples of the type are known to have survived: 5901, (MHA 901F), and 5905, (PHA 505G).

The S22 type was a reliable and well-liked vehicle and the class were well suited to their original duties working on the 'X' routes and as private hires when new. They were later employed on stage carriage services, where their specification was hardly altered. Passengers who saw a somewhat older vehicle turning up on their local route must have been pleasantly surprised when they sat back in the comfortable dual-purpose seats, which the buses retained until their withdrawal.

BMMO S23

The last buses to be designed and produced by BMMO were the seventy-six S23 single-decker buses. The S23s were built in two batches: 5916–5939, (RHA 916–39G), and 5940–5991, (UHA 940–991H), which entered service beginning December 1968. All buses up to 5941, which entered service on 5 January 1970, were completed at Carlyle Road Works. The last fifty, 5942–5991, were panelled and fitted out by Plaxton in Scarborough before returning to Carlyle Road for painting and pre-delivery inspection. Plaxton-finished examples had much longer interior roof panels than Carlyle finished ones but were otherwise identical. The last ever BMMO-built bus, the unpanelled integral frame of 5991, left the Central Works for Plaxtons on 27 February 1970 and finally entered service in July 1970.

The S23s were equipped with the by now standard BMMO 10.5-litre engine coupled to SCG four-speed semi-automatic gearbox. Again, the lessons of the braking system of the S17s were well learnt when the vehicles were used on intensive stage carriage work as disc brakes on the rear axle had given rise to excessive brake pad wear. As a result, the front axle had rubber-mounted independent suspension which was coupled to disc brakes on the front wheels, while the rubber suspension at the rear was coupled to drum brakes. A transmission handbrake was again used. Most of these buses were fitted with DPA fuel pumps rather than the CAV type previously standard – the type having previously been tested on 5901, one of the dual-purpose S22s.

Although having the same body shell as the earlier S21s and S22s, these vehicles were ordinary service buses with a B51F layout. They were of six-bay construction and could be distinguished from their immediate predecessors by having three top sliding ventilators on each side of the saloon in the first, third and fifth bays. All of these buses were fitted with rexine-covered bus seats with top grab rails, although 5916–5923 were briefly fitted with S17 type seats when new. They were then fitted with the correct type of seating beginning in March 1971. The buses had full-length luggage racks, fluorescent strip lighting and three centrally mounted Perspex opening roof ventilators.

Because of the impending winding-up of bus building at Carlyle Road and the loss of experienced coachbuilders, the construction of the S23s tended to use up any stock parts that could be fitted; this resulted in an amazing variety of unladen weights ranging from 6 tons 17½ cwt to 7¼ tons! Perhaps because of these problems, the quality of the S23s' bus bodywork always seemed poor and, after a period of time in service, the bodywork tended to be prone to defects. The difficulties in completing these buses resulted in a somewhat inferior build quality, which had not been seen on either of the earlier BMMO S21s and S22s. The Plaxton-finished examples were known for dropping the inner skin of the racks when in service and in later years both Carlyle and Plaxton models were patched up with plates to cover stress cracks on the inner roof panels, outer open panel lock areas and window pans.

The buses were, as was the usual practice for Midland Red, spread around the system's garages in generally ones, twos and threes, with Banbury, Bromsgrove, Coalville, Digbeth, Evesham, Hereford, Kidderminster, both Leicester garages, Lichfield, Ludlow, Redditch, Shrewsbury, Stafford, Sutton Coldfield, Swadlincote, Tamworth, Wellington, Wigston and Wolverhampton receiving examples when they were new.

The acquisition of Midland Red's services, 413 vehicles and assets in the Birmingham and Black Country area by West Midlands PTE on 3 December 1973 led to some twenty-four S23s passing to WMPTE. Five of the all-BMMO S23s, 5925, 5929, 5932, 5934 and 5938 were taken over, while nineteen of the Plaxton-finished examples, 5945-6, 5950-1, 5954-5, 5958, 5962, 5968-70, 5972-3, 5975, 5981-84 and 5986, were acquired. The first PTE withdrawals began in April 1978 while the last two, 5932 and 5981, went in January 1981. The first Midland Red-owned examples' withdrawal was in November 1979 and the class was decimated during the following year. As a result, the final member of the class, 5930, was finally withdrawn in early March 1981, having undertaken a ceremonial last journey from Leamington to Rugby with a specially made destination blind, reading: '1923–1981 Final Day of BMMO built buses'.

A number of S23s have survived. 5919, (RHA 919G), and 5941, (UHA 941H) – the last vehicle completely constructed by BMMO at their Central Works in Birmingham – are preserved, with bodies entirely completed at Carlyle Road's Central Work. Plaxton-finished examples 5956, 5963, 5969, 5977 and 5981, (UHA 956, 963, 969, 977 and 981H), are also preserved, and 5941 (in WMPTE livery) and 5956 and 5981 are located at Wythall. It was a great shame that 5991, (UHA991H) – the last vehicle to be built by BMMO – has been scrapped, despite being retained by MROC at their Central Works for a number of years due to its historical significance.

5841, JHA 841E

The conductor, wearing his Setright ticket machine, stands on the entrance step as 5841, (JHA 841E), passes through Coventry city centre when working on the X96 service to Northampton. This was a Leyland Leopard PSU3/4R that had entered service in March 1967 and was one of ten numbered 5839–5848. They were fitted with attractively proportioned Willowbrook DP49F bodies that were built to the standard BET Federation style with a wrap-around windscreen and rear windows, as well as four panoramic saloon windows. All ten were painted in the black-roofed dual-purpose livery and were converted to one-man operation in November 1970. (D. R. Harvey Collection)

5845, JHA 845E

Opposite above: Wearing the NBC poppy red livery is 5845, (JHA 845E), a Willowbrook DP49F-bodied Leyland Leopard PSU3/4R. It entered service in April 1967 as an LS20-classified vehicle from Coalville Garage, where it spent its entire life until its withdrawal. It is parked in Burton-on-Trent bus station, having arrived on the 668 service from Leicester bus station via Ashby-de-la-Zouch, and still retains its comfortable high-backed seats. The single-line destination box unfortunately only gave a limited amount of route information. (D. R. Harvey Collection)

5852, JHA 852E

Travelling along New Street, Birmingham, and passing the Marshall & Snelgrove department store, is BMMO S21 semi-coach 5852, (JHA 852E), in red and black coach livery. It is being used on the 107 service. 5852 had entered service on 7 April 1967 as one of thirty single-deckers intended for use on longer-distance stage carriage services in the week and coach duties at weekends with forty-nine blue-coloured semi-coach vinyl seats. It had a BMMO 10½-litre engine and SCG semi-automatic four-speed gearbox, with disc brakes all round and a transmission handbrake. The S21 was designed as a crew-operated vehicle. The basic body design was based on the BMMO CM6 six-bay motorway coach, with a BMMO S17-style windscreen, entrance door and emergency window, as well as a new curved front and rear dome and a single-piece rear window. The side windows were fixed and ventilation was by forced air through two roof scoops at the rear. It had the highly attractive front grille design that was only used on the S21 and had a large, two-door luggage compartment at the rear. (A. J. Douglas)

5870, LHA 870F

One of the nine S21s to pass to West Midlands PTE was 5870, (LHA 870F). It operated from new at Bromsgrove Garage in August 1967, before passing to WMPTE and operating from Harts Hill Garage. It is in the bus park in Dudley bus station while painted in WMPTE livery and, perhaps surprisingly, still retains its dual-purpose seating and the unique style of front grill. It was withdrawn in February 1979 and was bought for preservation, whereupon it was returned to its original red and black livery. (D. R. Harvey Collection)

5879, MHA 879F

The BMMO S22 was designed specifically for one-man operation use on long-distance stage carriage services. Mechanically, the BMMO S22 was identical to the S21, with a BMMO 10½-litre engine coupled to an SCG semi-automatic four-speed gearbox. The body had fixed side windows with forced air ventilation, rear luggage compartments and comfortable deep-cushioned, high-backed, red vinyl-covered bus seats. Their seating capacity was forty-five, with two large interior luggage pens replacing four seats behind the driver's cab. The first of the class, 5879, (MHA 879F), is parked in Shrewsbury bus station with the new-style radiator grill. (Vectis Publications)

5910, PHA 510G

Trundling through St Paul's bus station in Walsall is BMMO S22, 5910, (PHA 510G), which is working on the X8 express service to Birmingham on 5 April 1969. With its DP45F body, 5910 entered service on 19 September 1968. Built for long-distance stage carriage services, the S22s had a new design of front grill and included illuminated 'Pay As You Enter' signs at the front and yellow flip-over 'Limited Stop' signs at the side and rear. (A. J. Douglas)

5932, RHA 932G

Passing up the hill in Bagleys Lanes in Upper Gornal, Dudley, is 5932, (RHA 932G), a BMMO S23 with a Carlyle B51F body, which was new in April 1969. It passed to West Midlands PTE on 3 December 1973 and worked from Stourbridge Garage until it was withdrawn in January 1981. Behind it is the industrial landscape of factories and chimneys, as well as the vast tracts of derelict land that, in the early 1970s, still characterised this part of the Black Country. Since the mid-1980s this area has been transformed into a large residential area, with well over 400 houses built on concrete rafts over the reclaimed former mining land. Although the local bus route is still the 257, the road has been renamed Milking Bank. (D. R. Harvey Collection)

5941, UHA 941H

The BMMO S23 was a 36-foot-long, fifty-one seat single-decker bus designed for OMO. They had the same body shell as the S21s and S23s but were of six-bay construction. This one had an emergency window at the rear of the nearside of the saloon. 5941, (UHA 941H), was the last vehicle completely built by BMMO at Carlyle Works in Edgbaston, entering service in February 1970 from Banbury Garage. It is seen leaving Banbury bus station during its first year of service on the 500 service to Brackley via Middleton Cheney and Silverstone. 5941 was withdrawn in September 1980 and this historically important bus was sold for preservation. (R. H. G. Simpson)

5984, UHA 984H

The last fifty S23s were, mechanically, as advanced as Midland Red tradition had always demanded. They had BMMO horizontal 10.45-litre engines coupled to a four–speed semi-automatic gearbox and had Metalistic rubber suspension with servo-assisted disc brakes on the front wheels and drum brakes on the rear wheels. All fifty were sent to Plaxton for their bodywork to be completed. 5984, (UHA 984H), entered service in March 1970 and was allocated to Bearwood Garage after a few months. It was one of nineteen of the class to be transferred to WMPTE and was sent to the re-opened former BCT garage at Moseley Road. Not long after the takeover in 1974, 5984 is seen passing the 1930s-built Excelsior Hotel at the original entrance to Birmingham Airport. It is travelling along the A45 Coventry Road as it works on the 159 service from Birmingham to Coventry via Meriden. (D. Wilson)

Late BMMO-Purchased Single-Deckers

S25

6294–6393 (YHA 294–393J)

The reversion to traditional small-engined, lightweight buses in traditional Midland Red style harked back to the halcyon days of Wyndham Shire. Deliveries of the Leyland Leopards had fallen behind schedule and a large number of new vehicles needed to be acquired in a hurry. At the time, Ford were keen to secure large orders in the lightweight bus market and were willing to make BMMO a very attractive offer with short delivery times. The company were also keen to reduce operating costs and so BMMO placed an order with Don Everall (PSV) Limited of Wolverhampton in April 1970 for 100 examples of the Ford R192 fitted with B45F Plaxton Derwent 2 bodies.

The Ford was named the R192, after its 16 foot, or 192 inch, wheelbase, and could be fitted with 32-foot bodies that were capable of accommodating up to forty-five seats. All the Ford chassis operated by Midland Red were of the 192-inch wheelbase variation, which were fitted with the 141½ hp turbocharged diesel engine with a five-speed Clark gearbox. They were reclassified as F1 in 1974.

Numbered 6294–6393, (YHA 294–393J), the first vehicles were delivered just over six months later, and entered service as type S25s between November 1970 and June 1971. They were used on rural routes, which did not require large-capacity vehicles, and operated mainly form Banbury, Evesham, Hereford, Kineton, Ludlow, Rugby, Shrewsbury, Stratford-upon-Avon and Wellington garages. They had a number of shortcomings, with the engine cover restricting access to the lower saloon from the front entrance, as well as a quite awfully positioned gear lever. Their lightweight bodies were also only intended to have a short life and as they got older the bodywork became prone to structural weakness.

By September 1977, a number of Ford R192 type F1 buses were scheduled for disposal and as an experiment one such vehicle, fleet number 6391, (YHA391J), was taken to Midland Red's Central Works and shortened to make a twenty-seven seat midibus. The shortening work involved removing the whole body and shortening the chassis by cutting out sections from the wheelbase and behind the rear axle. To assist weight distribution, the fuel tank and batteries were moved to the rear. The original bodywork was overhauled and modified by having two whole bays removed from the relevant places, and the emergency door was moved to a new position in front of the offside rear wheel.

In all, seven type F1 Fords, 6360–6361 and 6388–6392, had been shortened by the end of 1979 and reclassified M2s, while two more, 6359 and 6362, had gone to Western National while 6393 passed to City of Oxford without being operated by Midland Red. Expected sales to other NBC companies never materialised, with only four orders being received. Considerable investment would have been made into converting these Fords but they proved to be underpowered for some of the work they were asked to do. As a result, the vehicle-shortening project was abandoned.

Normal withdrawals started in May 1977 and by the time of the breakup of Midland Red on 6 September 1981, only one bus, 6335, went to Midland Red (South) as a withdrawn bus, while Midland Red (North) operated 6325/36-9/45/50/3/67-74/82. 6372 and 6382 were the last to go, in January 1983. Remarkably, around sixty of the class were sold to other operators, though none survive in preservation.

S24

6394–6445 (YHA 394–417J, CHA 418–445K)

These fifty-two 36-ft-long Leyland Leopard PSU3A/2Rs with 18 foot 6 inch wheelbases were fitted with the large Leyland o.680 11.1-litre engine and a pneumocyclic gearbox. They had Willowbrook DP49F bodywork to the then standard BET Federation style and were delivered between April and December 1971. They were allocated mainly to the more rural garages away from the West Midlands and Leicester. The majority of the batch were divided between the four new bus operating companies on 6 September 1981. Those going to Midland Red (North) were withdrawn between January 1984 and October 1985, while those transferred to Midland Red (East) were withdrawn in a similar time frame. Sixteen went to Midland Red (South) on 6 September 1981. Withdrawals took place between February 1982 and January 1987, while the eleven sent to Midland Red (West) were taken out of service between October 1981 and December 1984.

S26

6461–6473 (DHA 461–473K)

These thirteen Leyland Leopard PSU3B/4Rs had Marshall B53F bodies built to the usual BET standard and were numbered 6461–6473, (DHA 461–473K). These were the last Midland Red buses to be numbered in the fleet number series instigated in 1944, which was retrospectively applied to the earlier bus fleet.

They entered service in May and June 1972 in full Midland Red livery. The 18 foot 6 inch wheelbase chassis was fitted with the 11.1-litre o.680 engine coupled to a semi-automatic pneumocyclic gearbox. Classified as S26, five went to Hinckley Garage and three went to Swadlincote. After the reformation of Midland Red on 6 September 1981, the eight that went to Midland Red (South) were withdrawn by March 1987, while the two that went to Midland Red (West) were withdrawn by October 1984. The final three of the class went to Midland Red (East) and the last one survived until January 1985.

CVC124C

About to turn out of Crocketts Road at the junction with Soho Road, Handsworth, is something of a rarity as far as Midland Red was concerned – a demonstrator! CVC124C was the second Daimler Roadliner SRC6 to reach the road and the first to be bodied as a bus. It was used by Midland Red during May and June 1968 and is being used on the 214 service. The attractive-looking Marshall B50F body belied the truly awful performance of the noisy, clanking Cummins V6-200 9.6-litre engine. Although Marshalls subsequently supplied bodies to Midland Red, the Roadliner went back to Coventry without any orders being placed. (A. E. Hall)

6299, YHA 299J

After the NBC takeover and the cessation of in-house bus building at Carlyle Road, in a further effort to reduce costs, 100 lightweight Ford R192s were ordered by BMMO in April via Don Everall (PSV) Limited of Wolverhampton, and were fitted with B45F Plaxton Derwent bodies. These were numbered 6294–6393, (YHA 294J–393J), and were classified as S25s, later becoming F1s. Intended to operate on rural services, many were based in the western and southern sides of Midland Red's operating area. A well-presented 6299, (YHA 299J), stands in Shrewsbury bus station wearing the NBC livery of poppy red and a single white band below the saloon windows, having arrived in the county town from Plox Green in Minsterley. The bus was new in November 1970 and spent its entire life at Shrewsbury Garage until it was withdrawn in September 1977. (J. G. Carroll)

6332, YHA 332J

The Ford designs were never considered to be very sophisticated, being quite basic but soundly engineered. They offered good value for money and were very popular with smaller operators, so it was quite surprising when BMMO placed their initial order for 100 vehicles in April 1970. All the Ford chassis operated by Midland Red were of the 192-inch wheelbase variation, fitted with the 5.9-litre turbocharged diesel engine, and these first hundred had a rather awkward Turner five-speed gearbox. On 23 April 1971, 6332, (YHA 332J), is just entering the High Street from Vine Street in Evesham and has just passed the Town Hall. The bus is about to take up its duty on the seventeen-minute-long short working to Cleeve Prior on the 148 service. The bus had entered service in December 1970 and was withdrawn in March 1980. (D. R. Harvey Collection)

6391, YHA 391J

New in March 1971 as a type S25, 6391, (YHA 391J), a Ford R192 with a Plaxton B45F body entered service at Evesham Garage and was withdrawn in September 1977. It was selected as one of the fifteen to be shortened to B27F at Carlyle Works in December 1977. 6391 was the first of the Fords to be shortened, which involved taking two central body bays out and the central section of the chassis to be reduced. The rear overhang was virtually removed, which produced a potentially useful bus that was bigger than the contemporary minibuses. Although these buses were offered to other NBC operators, only four went elsewhere, and the experiment was quickly abandoned. 6391 was sent to Redditch Garage and was reclassified M2. It is working on the R15 local service in Redditch bus station in the shadow of Kingfisher Shopping Centre, which dates from 1976. It was withdrawn in this condition in September 1980. (S. Knight)

6398, YHA 398J

Between April 1971 and December 1971, Midland Red purchased fifty-two Leyland Leopard PSU3A/4Rs, with Willowbrook DP49F bodywork, which had rear luggage boots. The dual-purpose seats were trimmed with leopard skin material and they were painted in an overall red BMMO bus livery with underlined 'Midland Red' fleet names. They were later repainted in the NBC dual-purpose livery of white and poppy red. 6398, (YHA 398J), is in its original livery in Smallbrook Ringway and is about to pass the entrance to New Street station. It is working on the X12 service from Derby via Burton-on Trent and Lichfield. New in May 1971 to Sutton Coldfield Garage, it was withdrawn early due to accident damage in August 1981. (J. G. Carroll)

6424, CHA 424K

Classified S24 by Midland Red, the Willowbrook dual-purpose Leyland Leopard PSU3A/Rs were frequently used when new on long-distance excursions and services. A nearly new 6424, (CHA 424K), allocated to Leamington Spa Garage, stands in an almost deserted Cardiff bus station on one such excursion. The disappointing feature of these otherwise pleasant buses was their lack of power steering, which made them hard work to drive. (D. R. Harvey Collection)

6461, DHA 461K

6461, (DHA 461K), sits in Pool Meadow bus station while its driver takes a short break 'on the cushions', having worked in from Leicester on the 658 route. The final thirteen buses bought by Midland Red before they restarted the fleet numbering system were a batch of Leyland Leopard PSU3A/4Rs with Marshall B53F bodywork, which were classified S26s. The first one of the batch, 6461, (DHA 461K), entered service in May 1972 from Hinckley Garage and was eventually transferred to Midland Red (South) on 6 September 1981. It was withdrawn in June 1984. (R. F. Mack)

6464, DHA 464K

Speeding along Bristol Street in Birmingham, having just crossed Smallbrook Ringway and with the Horsefair behind it, 6464, (DHA 464K), a Leyland Leopard PSU3A/4R with Marshall B53F bodywork, is working on the 147 route from Birmingham to Astwood Bank via Alvechurch in around 1980. What the destination display doesn't tell the intending passenger is that its main 'port of call' is Redditch! 6464 has the corporate NBC poppy red and white stripe livery. (D. R. Harvey)

NBC Single-Deckers

N1

101–158 (HHA 101–158L)

These were early versions of the integrally constructed Leyland National 1151/1R/2501 model. This meant that it was 11.3 metres long with an 8.3-litre straight-six turbo-charged Leyland 510 headless diesel engine powered at 200 bhp, coupled to a G2 five-speed gearbox. They had a single-front-entrance body and were right-hand drive. 101–107 were built with a B52F layout, being delivered to Midland Red in December 1972, but were re-seated to B51F before entering service – a layout that was standard for the rest of the class.

Internally, they were built to the drab, utilitarian Leyland National standard design, with seats in the front half that were too low to see above the bottom of the saloon windows, while those at the rear had to be climbed into after negotiating the steps in front of the rear axle. The driver's cab was well set out but the red, covered seats were not particularly comfortable for the passengers. These early Nationals had the long-style roof air-conditioning pod. Classified N1, these buses restarted the fleet number series at 101 and took the numbers up to 158.

The final four of the class entered service in August 1973, but seven of the buses, 148-154, barely lasted six months with Midland Red as they, along with twenty-seven others of the class, were transferred to West Midlands PTE on 3 December 1973. The WMPTE buses stayed in service until the company was privatised on 26 October 1986. After September 1981, of those that survived with Midland Red, twelve went to Midland Red (East), eleven went to Midland Red (West) and just two, 155–156, went to Midland Red (South). These two were withdrawn by July 1987, but Midland Red (East) and (West) examples were withdrawn in April 1990. 101, (HHA 101L), is preserved in the original Midland Red dark red livery.

F2

159–178 (HHA 159–178L)

Another twenty Ford R192s were purchased between December 1972 and January 1973. They were fitted with Plaxton Derwent 2 B45F bodies; these were the later R1014 models with the Ford four-speed synchromesh gearbox that was fitted to these F2 types. The first to be withdrawn was fleet number 163 in September 1979 and by the end of that November, all the remaining examples had been withdrawn – all with less than seven years' service. Most were sold for further use while six of those acquired by the dealer Paul Sykes were exported to Bangladesh in May 1981.

S27

199–248 (JHA 199–248L)

Fifty Leyland Leopard PSU3B/4Rs with Marshall DP49F bodies entered service from February to July 1973 and were painted in the dual-purpose Poppy Red livery of NBC with white above the waist rail and dual-purpose seats trimmed with leopard-skin-pattern material. They had rear luggage boots for long-distance work. Classified as S27s, these were attractive-looking single-deckers but were destined to have curtailed lives. On 6 September 1981, these buses were split between the four new constituent parts. Midland Red (East) took thirteen but all had been withdrawn in 1983. The Midland Red (North)'s fourteen buses were all withdrawn by April 1987. Midland Red (West) took only ten, with the last going in July 1987. The fourteen transferred to Midland Red (South) lasted the longest in service, with the last being withdrawn in December 1987. 227, 234 and 246, (JHA 227/ 234/246), have all been preserved.

N2

249– 298 (NHA 249–298M)

A further fifty Leyland National 1151/1R/2501 arrived between August 1973 and June 1974. They were also B51F bodywork with the exception of 295, which was delivered in June 1974 with a B49F layout. They differed from the first batch by having red vinyl-covered seats. While they were easy to access and, if well maintained, comfortable enough to ride in, the fixed-head 8.3-litre straight-six turbocharged Leyland 510 engine was noisy, prone to poor fuel consumption and was often very smoky if maintenance standards dropped. Fleet numbers 292–298 were built as Phase 2 specification by Leyland (chassis type 1151/1R), and these were delivered in June 1974.

Initial allocations of the N2 class included buses garaged at Worcester, Kidderminster, Redditch, Nuneaton, Stafford and Shrewsbury. All fifty buses passed to three of the four Midland Red companies in September 1981, with Midland Red (East) being the odd one out by not receiving any of the batch. Withdrawals began three years later and the last of the class were taken out of service in July 1990.

S28

319–368 (PHA 319–338M/SHA 639N/GJW 40–49N/GOH 350–361N)

Fifty more Leyland Leopard PSU3B/2Rs with standard BET-style Marshall DP49F bodywork were delivered over seven months between May and December 1974. They had dual-purpose seats trimmed with leopard skin material and had external rear luggage boots. They had NBC Poppy Red livery with white roofs and saloon window surrounds. They were numbered 319–368, but were registered with both 'M' and 'N' year-letter suffixes, as their delivery dates straddled the annual letter changeover on 1 August.

The first four of the class were used from new by Worcester Garage on the X43 and X44 express services to Birmingham via the M5 Motorway, though others were later used on an as-required basis. 320 was withdrawn due to fire damage in November 1978 and 329 was withdrawn after a severe accident in April 1977. The remaining forty-eight vehicles were reallocated in September 1981, with MR (East) getting fourteen, as did MR (South), while MR (North) got twelve and the remaining eight went to MR (West). All forty-eight buses were withdrawn between 1987 and 1996, though two buses, 354 and 323, lasted until 1995 and 1996 respectively. Three of the class, 319, (PHA 319M), 343, (GJW 43N), and 357, (GOH 357N), are preserved.

F3

369–388 (PHA 369–388M)

Between April and July 1974, Midland Red acquired another twenty Fords R1014s fitted with Plaxton Derwent 2 B45F bodywork. This was the final batch of Fords acquired by Midland Red and were classified as F3. They were allocated to Tamworth, Coalville, Wellington and Leamington garages. All were withdrawn between March 1980 and September 1981, though four F3 type Fords, fleet numbers 369–372, were shortened with a B27F layout by the end of 1979, being reclassified to type M3. The shortened buses were all withdrawn by 1982 and 370, (PHA 370M), having been converted to DP23F, is now preserved.

N3

389–438 (PHA 489–491M, GOL 392–438N)

These Leyland National 11351/1Rs, again with Leyland 510 fixed-head 8.3-litre engines, were delivered between July 1974 and October 1975 and had the reduced B49F layout pioneered by 295, (NHA 295M), but with light brown vinyl plastic-covered seating instead. These 11.3-metre-long buses mostly had the second shorter-length air-conditioning roof pod. 438, (GOL 438P), was new in August 1974 and was built as a joint venture with Avon CC as the 'Lifeliner' ambulance. It was exhibited at the 1974 Commercial Motor Show and was rebuilt in July 1975 to bus specification.

For 1975, the company had ordered ten Leyland Leopard coaches, ten Leyland Leopard dual-purpose buses, forty Bristol LH/ECW service buses and twenty Leyland Atlantean double-deck buses, but these were all cancelled by NBC, who overruled the Midland Red management and dictated that the Leyland National should become the standard vehicle for the company.

Unusually for Midland Red, these buses were allocated in groups; 389-391 went to Sandacre Garage in Leicester, 392–399 to Hereford, 400–405 to Tamworth, 406–413 to Rugby, 414–421 to Swadlincote, 422–427 to Wigston, 428–430 to

Redditch, 431–333 to Shrewsbury and 434–438 to Worcester. Most of these Nationals spent their entire Midland Red lives at their original garages. When the company split up on 6 September 1981, MR (East) got seventeen, which had all been sold on by 1986. MR (North) had ten, which succumbed almost en mass in April 1987. MR (South) received eight, which were nearly all withdrawn in April 1992, and MR (West) got fifteen, which were withdrawn by May 1990. From this batch only 403, (GOL 403N), was selected for an East Lancashire Greenway conversion, going to Northumbria as 714, (PDZ 6278), in January 1995. 436, (GOL 436N), is now preserved.

N4

471–501 (JOX 471–501P)

This batch of thirty buses were more Leyland National Mk 1 11351A/1Rs, with the standard layout and light brown seating in a B49F configuration, and were the last of Midland Red's Leyland Nationals to have chrome handrails and fittings. These buses and all subsequent Mk 1 Nationals had a shorter air-conditioning pod. They were delivered between October 1975 and May 1976 as Midland Red N4 types.

Again, the more rural and country town garages received allocations of these Leyland Nationals. Garages such as Leamington, Nuneaton, and Coalville, Kidderminster, Shrewsbury and Redditch got small batches, as well as the same garages that had members of the previous class. Eight were taken over by Midland Red (East) and were withdrawn between March 1986 and May 1989. Midland Red (North) got eleven, one of which survived until December 1998, some eleven years after their first withdrawal, and twelve went to Midland Red (West), whose buses were sold to WMPTE in May 1994. From this batch, six buses were subsequently selected for East Lancashire Greenway conversions.

N5

502–535 (JOX 501–535P)

Banbury, Hinckley, Stafford and Redditch garages had deliveries of these thirty-four Leyland National Mk1 11351A/1Rs, which again had B49F bodywork. They were all delivered between July 1976 and September 1976 with light brown seats and went to garages at Banbury, Herford, Shrewsbury, Wigston, Tamworth and Kidderminster. None had been transferred from their first garage by the time of the break-up of Midland Red on 6 September 1981.

Midland Red (East) received six buses and Midland Red (North) got eleven, all of which were withdrawn or transferred to one of the other constituents by June 1983. Midland Red (South) only got four, which were withdrawn over a seven-year period. Finally, Midland Red (West) received ten of this batch, as well as some transferred from Midland Red (East); ten of this group were sold to West Midlands PTE in August 1995, though most were withdrawn after about twelve months. From this batch only 516, (JOX 516P), was selected for an East Lancashire Greenway conversion in August 1994. One of this class, 506, (JOX 506P), was purchased for preservation in 2002.

N6

536–610 (NOE 536–610R)

This order of seventy-five buses was for Leyland National Mk 1 11351A/1Rs with B49F layouts. They were delivered between August 1976 and May 1977. The main recipients were Leamington with eighteen, Worcester with twelve, and Hinckley with ten, while garages at Coalville, Nuneaton, Redditch and Shrewsbury all received small numbers. Yet again, these Leyland Nationals were not allocated to either the West Midlands or Leicester areas.

On the split-up of Midland Red into four constituent parts on 6 September 1981, the new Midland Red (East) only got ten of this batch, while Midland Red (South) received thirty-three. Both Midland Red (North) and South acquired sixteen each. The earliest withdrawals took place in 1987 from Midland Red (North), while Midland Red (South) had a few that lingered on until February 1992. From this batch, three Leyland National Mk I buses were selected for an East Lancashire Greenway conversion and two of this batch, 544, (NOE 544R), and 602, (NOE 602R), were bought for preservation in 1997 and 2004 respectively.

N7

617–664 (PUK617–656R/SOA 657–664S)

Another forty-eight Leyland National 11351A/1Rs with B49F bodywork entered service between March 1977 and February 1978. While the Leyland National was capable of a good top speed and excellent acceleration, it was often too large for the only jobs left for it to do. On Midland Red's out of town and rural services they just pootled around country back roads for which they were never designed and were totally unsuited. As there was virtually no alternative single-deck model being built by Leyland's subsidiaries yet more Mk 1 Nationals were purchased.

Garages at Tamworth, Wigston, Kidderminster and Swadlincote were supplied with members of this class, though a few were delivered to Sandacre Street in Leicester. After barely four years' service with Midland Red, the class was split up, with Midland Red (East) getting seventeen, Midland Red (North) getting eight, Midland Red (South) getting ten and Midland Red (West) getting thirteen. The Midland Red (East) ones had all gone by about 1990 and the Midland Red (North) ones by October 1987, while all ten of Midland Red (South) were fitted with DAF engines.

Fourteen of the class were sold to West Midlands PTE in the spring of 1994, though they only had a service life of about two years. From this batch, East Lancashire reconstructed four buses for Greenway conversion, although all came back to the Midland Red group. 656, (SOA 656S), was bought for preservation in 2002.

N8

683–724 (TOF 683–719S/WOC 720–725T)

Forty-two Leyland National 11351A/1R buses with a B49F layout were delivered to Midland Red between April 1978 and December 1978. Their layout was exactly the same as the previous batch, with short-length air-conditioning pods and spartan interiors, although they had high-level luggage rack on the offside.

Wellington Garage received a total of twenty-six of this batch, numbered 683–705/717–9, while Banbury, Bromsgrove and Wigston garages all had three or four each. 686 had its roof pod removed in November 1988 for use on the 825 service, but it was destroyed in a fire four years later, along with nineteen other buses at Stafford Garage in February 1992. 706 must have been Midland Red's shortest-lived Leyland National as it was written off after overturning in October 1978, after only being in service for eighty-four days. All of Wellington's buses passed to Midland Red (North), while Midland Red (East), (South) and (West) received seven, five and four buses respectively. All the Midland Red (East) ones had been withdrawn by June 1994, while all the Midland Red (North) and (West) buses had been taken out of service by June 2000, leaving just 710 with Midland Red (South) to soldier on until August 2002.

From this batch, only 694, TOF 694S, was selected for an East Lancashire Greenway conversion, and this went to Midland Red (North) in March 1995.

N9

742–773 (XOV 742–760T/BVP 761–773V)

The final delivery for Mk 1 Leyland National 11351A/1Rs with B49F bodywork was for thirty-two buses, which arrived between February 1979 and January 1980. These were some of the last Mk 1 Nationals to be built with 772 and 773 being two of the only ten to enter service during 1980. Uniquely, they all had dark brown seats, a high-level luggage rack on the offside and black handrails and fittings.

By this time, the Leyland Motors policy of having one bus that operators had to use in a variety of unsuitable roles was beginning to wear a little thin. The four Midland Red companies would soon turn to high-floor Leyland Tiger TL11s buses or, in the case of Midland Red (West), to the Leyland Lynx LX bus.

Bromsgrove and Redditch garages each got six buses, Leamington four and Wellington got three, but the rest were scattered around in ones and twos to Tamworth, Cannock, Rugby Nuneaton and Evesham. After a short career with Midland Red, after 6 September 1981 Midland Red (North) received ten buses, Midland Red (South) seven and Midland Red (West) fifteen. Seven of the buses were sold to West Midlands PTE in 1994, mostly from MR (West), who took ten years (between February 1990 and November 2000) to eliminate their allocation. Midland Red (North)'s final withdrawal occurred in July 2002, when 763, (BVP 763V), was taken out of service and sold for preservation. The last of Midland Red (South)'s buses went in November 2001.

N10

807–831 (BVP 807–822V/EON 823–831V)

The National 2 was introduced in 1979. It differed from its predecessor mainly in its having a bulbous grille and a front-mounted radiator. These were the last buses delivered to Midland Red and were the only Leyland National 2116L11/1Rs delivered before the break-up of the company in September 1981.

In 1979, Midland Red Omnibus Company Limited (MROC) placed an order for forty new Leyland National 2 single-deck buses, (fleet numbers 807–847), though only twenty-five buses arrived due to financial problems. The N10 vehicles were built to 'B' series specification, with dark brown seats and were fitted with under-floor heaters instead of a roof-mounted heating pod. They had the more conventional Leyland 0.680 11.6-litre engine without a turbocharger.

These twenty-five Leyland National 2s had B49F bodywork and were delivered between January and June 1980, being allocated to Kidderminster, Nuneaton, Stafford, Shrewsbury, Southgate Street in Leicester, Tamworth and Wigston garages, with each getting between two and five buses each. They had hardly been run in when the garages were each attached to one of the four new operating companies, resulting in eight becoming the property of Midland Red (East), with twelve going to the Midland Red (North), Midland Red (South) getting four and Midland Red (West) just two.

As a class, they were not long-lived; the Midland Red (East) ones all went by July 1999, the Midland Red (North) ones went by June 1994, while the last of Midland Red (South)'s Leyland National 2s went in July 1999. Both of the Midland Red (West) buses were sold to the associated Badgerline Company of Weston-Super-Mare in May 1989. 830, (EON 830V), was fitted with a nearside wheelchair lift and was re-seated to DP39FL in May 1985. Only one Leyland National 2 was rebuilt by Easy Lancs to a Greenway conversion. 808, (BVP 808V), and 811, (BVP 811V), were both purchased for preservation, in 2001 in 2003 respectively.

101, HHA 101L

Overleaf above: Parked at the Imperial War Museum site in Duxford at the Showbus Rally on 26 September 2010 is Midland Red 101, (HHA 101L). This was the company's first Leyland National and was a 1151/1R/2501 Mk 1 model. This was the first of a batch of fifty-eight vehicles; they had fifty-two seats and single entrance doors and were Leyland's first major order for the single-door version. 101 had the distinction of being the only Leyland National to be delivered in the traditional Midland Red livery. It was built in October 1972 and entered service after two months, being used for familiarisation duties. (D. R. Harvey)

113, HHA 113L

Overleaf below: 113, (HHA 113L), was one of thirty-three of this first N1 class of Leyland Nationals to be taken over by WMPTE on 3 December 1973, but never got beyond the red fablon WM sticker livery stage as it was withdrawn in July 1974 after being damaged by fire. It is in St Martin's Circus and is turning in front of the Rotunda into High Street before turning into New Street, where the 113 city centre terminus was located. The bus would then travel to the Hardwick Arms, Sutton Coldfield. (D. R. Harvey Collection)

120, HHA 120L

As a Hillman Hunter pulls away, Midland Red Leyland National 120, (HHA 120L), stands in Malvern in 1981 when about to work on the 344 route back to Worcester. It entered service in March 1973 and was re-seated to a B51F layout when just one month old. It eventually passed to Midland Red (West) at the formation of the new company on 6 September 1981 and lasted another ten years in service. (D. R. Harvey Collection)

151, HHA 151L

A somewhat mud-splattered 151, (HHA 151L), is parked in Stourbridge bus station on 19 January 1985 when working on the 556 route back to Wolverhampton. The Leyland National in the distance is parked near the entrance to the bus station, which stood at the end of a fearsome climb from Stourbridge Ring Road. This Leyland National 1151/1R/2501 was one of the thirty-three vehicles from this batch to be transferred to WMPTE with the local Black Country BMMO services and assets. Renumbered in September 1982 to 5151, this Harts Hill Garage bus was withdrawn in August 1986. (D. R. Harvey)

168, HHA 168L

An interloper in the camp! On 23 November 1975, 168, (HHA 168L), a Ford R1014 with a 5.9-litre turbocharged diesel engine, a Ford four-speed synchromesh gearbox and a Plaxton Derwent B45F body, dating from December 1972, has escaped from its home garage at Kidderminster. Classified as an F2 by Midland Red, it stands in Stourbridge bus station having worked on the 311 service via Blakedown and Hagley. It was virtually the same as the F1 Fords except for the gearbox. 168 was withdrawn in November 1979 and was exported to Bangladesh in May 1981. (E. V. Trigg)

176, HHA 176L

A Plaxton Derwent II-bodied Ford R1014 with a B45F layout is parked in Shrewsbury bus station when working on the local town service S13 service to Copthorne. This bus is loading up with passengers as the driver is issuing tickets from his cab-mounted Setright ticket machine. The bus had entered service in January 1973 and was withdrawn in November 1979. This second batch of twenty Fords seemed to have much shorter service lives that the larger batch of 100, possibly because they only had four-speed gearboxes. (J. G. Carroll)

205, JHA 205L

Turning onto the A45 at about 2 p.m. from the original entrance to the then Elmdon Airport in front of the Excelsior Hotel is 205, (JHA 205L). New in February 1973 as type S27, and originally allocated to Sutton Coldfield Garage, it is working on the X96. There were only two full through journeys each weekday, as it travelled on the five hour and forty minute journey from Shrewsbury to Northampton via Wolverhampton, Birmingham, Coventry and Rugby. This Leyland Leopard PSU3/2R was one of fifty that entered service between February 1973 and July 1973. Fitted with forty-nine leopard skin moquette-trimmed seats and a luggage boot, these vehicles were well suited to the company's longer journeys. (D. Wilson)

236, JHA 236L

236, (JHA 236L), turns into the Parade in Leamington Spa when working on the 591 route from Coventry and Warwick on 4 April 1976. This Leyland Leopard PSU3.2R had the usual 9.8-litre horizontal 0.600 engine coupled to a Pneumocyclic gearbox and had an 18 foot 6 inch chassis wheelbase. The BET-style body was a Marshall DP49F unit and was, overall, 35 feet 1½ inches long. It was delivered in the NBC poppy red and white dual-purpose livery in May 1973. (A. D. Packer)

254, NHA 254M

Having been taken over by Midland Red (West) on 6 September 1981, 254, (NHA 254M), new in August 1973 to Worcester Garage, emerges into Edgbaston Street, Birmingham, from the underground gloom of the bus station, located below the Bull Ring Centre, on 11 February 1989. The attractive livery and old-fashioned style of fleet name helped to mask the slab sides of this Leyland National 1151/1R/2501. It would be withdrawn just fifteen months later, having spent its entire life working from Worcester Garage. This batch of fifty buses was classified by Midland Red as type N2. (D. R. Harvey)

269, NHA 269M

From 1981 until 1985, 269, (NHA 269M), during its ownership by Midland Red (South), was allocated to Banbury Garage. Travelling into Banbury town centre is Leyland National 1151/1R/2501 with a B52F body that was new in November 1973 and which was quickly reduced by one in order to provide a luggage rack. These buses had the long air ventilation pod on the roof and were classified N2 by the company. (D. R. Harvey Collection)

321, PHA 321M

Negotiating the traffic alongside the row of Georgian properties in Bridge Street in Stratford-upon-Avon is 321, (PHA 321M), a Leyland Leopard PSU3B/2R new in May 1974. It was the third vehicle in a batch of fifty vehicles that were built with DP49F Marshall bodywork and were classified S28s. The bus is working on the 502 town service to the nearby village of Shottery – the fifteenth-century childhood home of Ann Hathaway, who was to become William Shakespeare's wife. (D. R. Harvey Collection)

364, GOL 364N

Wearing the somewhat flashy red, yellow and white Midland express livery is 364, (GOL 364N). New in January 1975 as type S28, this Leyland Leopard PSU3B/2R is actually owned by Midland Fox and is negotiating Belgrave Gate in Leicester city centre. The bus has a Marshall DP49F body and it is working on the X66 express service to Birmingham via the M69 and Coventry. The bus was withdrawn in November 1986. (D. R. Harvey Collection)

369, PHA 369M

In 1974, MROC acquired another twenty R1014 Fords and, like all the previous Fords ordered by Midland Red, these were fitted with Plaxton Derwent bodywork and B45F seating. This was the final batch of Fords acquired by Midland Red and they entered service from April 1974, being classified as Midland Red type F3s. New in April 1974, 369, (PHA 369M), went to Tamworth Garage until it was withdrawn in March 1979 and converted from type F3 to type M3, while being shortened to a B27F layout. It was finally withdrawn for good in November 1980. It is seen working on the 791 service to the 1890s colliery village of Wood End. (D. R. Harvey Collection)

383, PHA 383M

383, (PHA 383M), is standing outside the Tontine Hotel in the famous Coalbrookdale town of Ironbridge when working on the 920 service, though it lacks, somewhat typically for the NBC era, any destination blinds. 383, a Ford R1014, had a Paxton B45F body and entered service from Wellington Garage. The hotel is named after the eighteenth-century practice of a tontine agreement, which effectively meant that a group partnership would be inherited by 'the last man standing'. Notoriously, this led to murders, and such agreements were eventually made illegal. (D. R. Harvey)

390, PHA 490M

Passing along Humberstone Gate and about to turn into Charles Street in Leicester is 390, (PHA 490M), while employed on the 651 service to Barkby. This Leyland National 11351/1R was the second bus in a class of fifty classified as N3 and had a B49F layout. Only the first three of these N3s came with the original style of long roof air ventilator pods. It had been new in August 1974 to Wigston Garage and is seen in the final Midland Red livery before passing to Midland Red (East). It was an early withdrawal, as it was sold in July 1983 to Provincial of Gosport. (A. J. Douglas)

406, GOL 406N

Parked in Pool Meadow bus station in Coventry is Leyland National 11351/1R 406, (GOL 406N), with the Central Swimming Baths in Fairfax Street, opened in 1966, behind it. It is working on the 596 service to the village of Napton some 3 miles east of Southam in Warwickshire. Delivered in March 1975 to Rugby Garage, it came fitted with the newer, smaller roof heating pod. It passed to Midland Red (South), while still allocated to Rugby, and was withdrawn during November 1990. (A. J. Douglas)

484, JOX 484P

Turning into Redditch bus station, with the railway station entrance beyond the railings on the left, is 484, (JOX 484P). It is working on the R8 Matchborough circular town service, a large part of which incurred driving on a 'Buses Only' road absolutely flat-out in order to keep time. It was a nightmare! 484 was a Leyland National 11351/1R Mk 1, Phase 2, and was one of the batch of thirty-one buses. It was built with a B49F layout and a short-length roof heating pod, having the class code N4. It is wearing the Reddibus livery that was applied to most of the Nationals allocated to Redditch Garage. (A. J. Douglas)

506, JOX 506P

Standing in the bus parking area at the Bass Brewery Museum in Burton-on-Trent is preserved Leyland National 11351A/1R Mk 1 506, (JOX 506P), which is wearing the NBC poppy red version of the Midland Red (South) livery with a white stripe at cantrail level and the shorter roof heating pod. It had entered service as one of thirty-four in the July 1976 batch. Classified N5 by the company, the batch was delivered with a small ventilation pod and a light-brown-seated B49F layout with black handrails. 506 was withdrawn in September 1995 and passed to the Birmingham Coach Co. Ltd, Birmingham, with whom it ran until April 2002. It is at the Burton Bus Rally on 30 July 2005 and behind it is the author's preserved former Birmingham City Transport Crossley-bodied Crossley DD42/6 2489, (JOJ 489). (D. R. Harvey)

629, PUK 629R

Leyland National 11351A/1R Mk 1 629, (PUK 629R), coded N6 by Midland Red, was one of a large batch of seventy-five B49F models. The Leyland National was a concoction of opposites; the body style could hardly be called attractive and it was hardly comfortable for the passengers, yet it was functional and immensely strong. A 'good' National was easy to drive, yet with its fixed head, noisy and polluting engine, it was a mechanics nightmare! 629 went into service in May 1977 and is working the interurban 591 service to Warwick and Coventry. The bus is in the standard NBC livery and is leaving the Bridgefoot bus station in Stratford–upon-Avon. (A. J. Douglas)

698, TOF 698S

Having entered service in April 1978 from Wellington Garage, Leyland National 11351A/1R Mk 1 698, (TOF 698S), was classified N8 by Midland Red. It was one of forty-two vehicles, numbered 683–724, that entered service between April 1978 and December 1978 with the short-length roof heating pod. The forty-nine light brown seats had a luggage rack above them on the offside. It is working a Bridgnorth Town Service and is parked in High Street just beyond the junction with Church Street in High Town on 1 April 1985. (D. R. Harvey)

752, XOV 752T

Travelling down Hill Street on 11 February 1989, towards the left turn into Station Street and then into the gloom of Birmingham's Bull Ring bus station, is 752, (XOV 752T). Behind the bus is the Futurist Cinema, which was the first in the city to be equipped for sound films. By now owned by Midland Red (West), 752 is working on the 131 route. This was one of the final deliveries of Mk 1 Leyland National 11351A/1Rs with B49F bodywork, entering service in April 1979. They were classified as N9, although they were basically the same as the previous N8s. This was the first vehicle repainted in the red and cream bus livery in October 1986 and was allocated to Digbeth Garage. (D. R. Harvey)

764, BVP 764V

The fleet name 'Chaserider' was used by Midland Red (North) for their services in the Cannock area. Parked in High Green, Cannock, while working on the 860 route is 764, (BVP 764V), a B49F-bodied Leyland National 11351A/1R with the smaller roof heating pod that was new in November 1979. It was equipped with dark brown seats, black handrails and fittings, and a high-level luggage rack on the offside. The bus was taken over by Midland Red (North) on 6 September 1981 and was withdrawn in February 1998. (D. R. Harvey Collection)

818, BVP 818V

In 1979, Midland Red Omnibus Company Limited (MROC) placed an order for forty 11.6m Leyland National 2 single-deck buses with fleet numbers 807–847. Unfortunately, by the time deliveries started, MROC were in such grave financial difficulties that the order had to be reduced to just twenty-five buses, which were numbered 807–831. Classified as N10s, 818, (BVP 818V), entered service in April 1980 from Nuneaton Garage. It passed to Midland Red (South) after the breaking-up of the Midland Red company on 6 September 1981 and was finally withdrawn in September 1995. It is standing in Nuneaton bus station when working on the N48 Nuneaton Town service to Chapel End. (D. R. Harvey Collection)

830, EON 830V

Parked in St Margaret's bus station in Leicester is 830, (EON 830V). This Leyland National 2 NL116L11/1R was new in June 1980 and is wearing its original NBC livery. The Mk 2 version of the Leyland National featured a restyled front, incorporating a front-mounted radiator. To further save money, these vehicles were built to 'B' series specification; being fitted with under-floor heaters instead of a roof-mounted heating pod, and the standard version of the Leyland L11 8.2-litre engine, without a turbocharger. (R. H. G. Simpson)

1970s Takeovers

Stratford Blue

The history of Stratford Blue Motors is somewhat convoluted, but its origin was in the Leamington & Warwick Motor Omnibus Company, who first ran a bus service from Kenilworth in 1905. The Balfour Beatty-owned Leamington & Warwick Company purchased the small Stratford-upon-Avon Motor Services operation on 15 March 1929. After L&W had purchased twelve Daimler CF6s with Brush bodies to replace the tram service between those two towns, Stratford–upon-Avon Blue Motors was formed on 4 May 1931, being financed by Balfour Beatty. Control of Stratford Blue was taken on by BMMO on 30 June 1935 and, in 1947, the control of ordering new buses passed into the hands of the Stratford Blue management, who purchased a new single-decker fleet, starting with Leyland Tiger PS1s, PS2/1s and PS2/3 between 1947 and 1950, which eliminated all of the second-hand pre-war fleet. After 1954, underfloor-engined Leyland Tiger Cubs and Leyland Leopards became the standard choice for single-deck bus work.

The takeover of Midland Red by the National Bus Company was caused by the BET Group deciding to sell its interests in road transport in March 1969. Stratford-upon-Avon Blue Motors were closed down, being absorbed by Midland Red on 1 January 1971. Midland Red took over the bus fleet and the two garages at Stratford and Kineton. The single-deck buses taken over on 1 January 1970 were three groups of Leyland Tiger Cub PSUC1/1s, as well as two Leyland Leopards.

2040–2044 (2741–2745 AC)
Originally numbered 40–44 in the Stratford Blue fleet, these Leyland Tiger Cub PSUC1/1s had Willowbrook bodywork, with the first four being DP41F, while 44 had a B45F body. They were delivered in January and February 1959. All were sold to Potteries MT in June 1971 as their 401–405.

2045–2048 (3945–3948 UE)
These Leyland Tiger Cub PSUC1/1s were Stratford Blue's 45–48 and had Park Royal B45F bodywork. They were delivered during November 1960. All were sold to Potteries MT in May 1971 as their 406–409. 45 was subsequently sold for preservation.

2049–2053 (5449–5452/5455 WD)
These five single-deckers were bodied by Marshall, with the first one being fitted as a B43F bus and the remaining four as DP41Fs. The last one, 2053, also had a two-speed

back axle. They were delivered between February and May 1962 as Stratford Blue's 49–52 and 55, and were renumbered 49–53 in December 1970. They were withdrawn without ever being painted in Midland Red livery.

2054 (CWD33C)
This was a Leyland Leopard PSU3/3R with a Weymann B53F body that was delivered in January 1965 and was numbered 60 until December 1970. It ran with Midland Red until May 1976 and was one of the first Leyland Leopards in the fleet to be broken up.

2059 (HAC628D)
A Marshall DP41F Leyland Leopard L2T that was delivered in June 1966 as their 62. It was renumbered 59 in December 1970 and ran with Midland Red until May 1978, when it was converted to a dual-control driver tuition vehicle. It remained as such, having been transferred to MR (West) on 6 September 1981, until it was withdrawn after a gearbox failure in April 1992. It was sold for preservation in April 1995 and was restored as Stratford Blue's 62.

Harper Brothers, Heath Hayes

2247 (NRF 420L)
This was a Bedford SB5 with a front-mounted Bedford 5.42-litre engine. It had a lightweight Willowbrook B40F bodywork with an entrance immediately behind the front axle and was new in October 1972. This was the only single-deck bus taken over from Harper Brothers, which occurred on 7 September 1974.

G. Cooper, Oakengates

G. Cooper of Oakengates ran in their services as part of the Shropshire Omnibus Association in the Donnington and Oakengates services. At its peak, as many as eighteen independent bus operators pooled their resources in this east Shropshire area. Coopers sold out to the predatory Midland Red on 15 October 1973. Only four vehicles from the Coopers fleet were operated and all of their remaining coach fleet was sold.

2140–2141 (FAW 156–157D)
New in January 1966, these two Bedford VAM5s had front mounted Bedford 5.42-litre Diesel engine and Duple B45F bodies and both were sold to City of Oxford MS as their 616 and 617 in February 1975.

2144 (UUJ 447J)
New in March 1971, 2144 was a Bedford YRQ with a Willowbrook DP45F body. It was sold to City of Oxford MS as their 59 in February 1975.

2145 (VNT 848J)

This Bedford YRQ was new in July 1971 and also had a Willowbrook DP45F body. It was sold to City of Oxford MS as their 60 in February 1975.

T. Hoggins & Sons, Wrockwardine Wood

On 6 January 1974, BMMO took over the business of Hoggins, Wrockwardine Wood, Shropshire. The fleet numbered five, only one of which was a bus and that was duly operated in the Midland Red fleet.

2181 (XUX 417K)

This was a Ford R192 with a B47F Plaxton Derwent body. It had a similar specification to the type F1 Fords already operated and, after receiving Midland Red-style destination displays and the standard 'Poppy Red' livery, re-entered service with Midland Red at Heath Hayes Garage. It later saw service at Kidderminster and Redditch garages before being withdrawn in December 1978.

43, (2744 AC)

On hire to Midland Red, 43, (2744 AC), has arrived in Victoria coach station and is parked alongside a pair of Standerwick Weymann-bodied Leyland Atlantean PDR1/1 double-deck coaches. 43 was a Leyland Tiger Cub PSUC1/1s with a Willowbrook DP41F body, delivered in February 1959. All were sold to Potteries MT in June 1971 immediately after the Midland Red takeover. (R. H. G. Simpson)

45, (3945 UE)

There were four Leyland Tiger Cub PSUC1/1 single-deckers delivered to Stratford Blue during November 1960 and, quite unusually for the company, they had B45F bodywork rather than being fitted with dual-purpose seating. The body was built by Park Royal. The first one, 45, (3945 UE), is parked alongside the Red Lion public house at Bridgefoot bus station after it had been converted to OMO. It was numbered 2045 after the Midland Red takeover and was subsequently sold for preservation. (R. Marshall)

55, (5455 WD)

Five more Leyland Tiger Cub PSUC1/1 single-deckers were bodied by Marshall, with the first one being fitted as a B43F bus and the remaining four as DP41Fs. The last one, 55, (5455 WD), also had a two-speed back axle and was delivered in May 1962. It is in Shipston-on-Stour, which was almost halfway along the 44 route between Stratford and Oxford. It was renumbered 53 in April 1969. They were withdrawn without ever being painted in Midland Red livery in April 1971. (D. R. Harvey Collection)

60, (CWD33C)

60, (CWD33C), a Leyland Leopard PSU3/3R with a Weymann B53F body, was delivered in January 1965 to Stratford Blue and was renumbered 54 in August 1969. It is standing in Gloucester Green bus station, Oxford, prior to working on the 44 route back to Stratford. Although nominally a bus it had comfortable, high-backed seats. It ran with Midland Red until May 1976. (R. H. G. Simpson)

2059, (HAC628D)

Standing on the forecourt of Kineton Garage is 62, (HAC 628D). It was a Marshall DP41F Leyland Leopard L2T, which was delivered in June 1966 as their 62 and was renumbered 59 in December 1970. It ran with Midland Red as 2059 until May 1978, when it was converted to a dual-control driver tuition vehicle. It was transferred to Midland Red (West) on 6 September 1981 and was finally withdrawn in April 1992. It was sold for preservation in April 1995 and restored as Stratford Blue 62. (D. R. Harvey Collection)

2247, (NRF 420L)

This was a Bedford SB5 with a front-mounted Bedford 5.42-litre engine. It had lightweight Willowbrook B40F bodywork with an entrance immediately behind the front axle. This was the only single-deck bus taken over from Harper Brothers and was new to them in October 1972 as their 47. It was repainted into NBC poppy red livery in February 1975 and was withdrawn in January 1977. It is at The Circle in Kingstanding and is about to return to Heath Hayes from where it spent its entire life. (D. R. Harvey Collection)

2141, (FAW 157D)

Coopers sold out to the predatory Midland Red on 15 October 1973. Only four vehicles from the Coopers fleet were operated and all their remaining coach fleet was sold. New in January 1966, 2141, (FAW 157D), was the second of a pair of Bedford VAM5s with Duple B45F bodies with an front entrance alongside the low-mounted Bedford 5.42-litre diesel engine and the set-back axles. The bus stands opposite the Cock Hotel in Wellington. Both of the pair were sold to City of Oxford MS in February 1975. (R. H. G. Simpson)

2145, (VNT 848J)

2145, (VNT 848J), a Bedford YRQ, was new in July 1971 and also had a Willowbrook DP45F body. It was similar to their previous bus, 2144, (UUJ 447J). Although rather spartan, they were well suited for the village services in East Shropshire. It was sold to City of Oxford MS as their 60 in February 1975 and is parked in the COMS garage yard. (R. H. G. Simpson)

2181, (XUX 417K)

Standing at The Circle in Kingstanding is the by now Midland Red 2181, (XUX 417K). This Plaxton Derwent B47F-bodied Ford R192 was new in 1972 and was the only modern single-decker in the Hoggins of Wrockwardine Wood fleet at the time of their takeover in January 1974. It was virtually the same as Midland Red's own Ford R192s. (D. R. Harvey Collection)

A Last Overview

These were the last SOS and BMMO marques designed, manufactured and operated by Midland Road at their Carlyle Road Works in Edgbaston. From 1923, when the Standard SOS, based on a Tilling-Stevens-designed chassis, better known as the S type, was first introduced in 1923, until the final withdrawals from service in March 1981, the Birmingham & Midland Motor Omnibus Company and its successors produced a series of double-decker and single-decker buses, as well as a fleet of successful coaches that all had the same characteristics. They were fast, economical, lightweight and, frequently, sufficiently mechanically advanced as to make 'mainstream' chassis manufacturers wince at the sheer bravado of an operating company building their own design of PSV, which was in advance of their own products.

It was only twelve years after Midland Red began to produce their own chassis that, in 1935–6, the four advanced REC rear-engined single-deckers went into service. All four RECs were converted between 1941 and 1944 to an underfloor-engined chassis layout. A further pre-production single-decker prototype followed in 1946. Thus, the production of the post-war S series began at the end of 1946 and gave Midland the 'jump' on virtually all the big players in the manufacturing of underfloor-engined single-deckers by at least three and a half years.

It was amazing that an operating company could keep on improving and refining the breed by employing, from the early 1950s onward, integral construction, disc brakes, independent suspension and the extensive use of fibreglass in the bodywork. At the time, AEC, Leyland, Guy and later Daimler were all wedded to over-engineered, though robust, heavyweight chassis. When bodied, these first underfloor-engined chassis could reach around 8½ tons. AEC, Leyland and Guy soon began to produce lightweight chassis in an attempt to reduce fuel consumption and were briefly joined by products manufactured by Albion and Atkinson.

Meanwhile, Midland Red was beginning to achieve a complete integral bus, which weighed in at little over 5 tons. This was the S14 service bus, which was both amazing and yet 'a bridge too far', as, being cut down to the bone, the vehicles were neither pleasant to drive nor pleasant to ride in. Not all early, shorter, post-war S classes were good; some were quite poor and yet others were superb. In the first category were the service buses, the S8s, S9s, S10s and S12s, while the S13 dual-purpose buses (the last single-deckers to be built with chassis) were, although distinctly heavyweight, excellent vehicles. The contrast between the lightweight S14s and the excellent dual-purpose S15s could not have been more apparent. Once BMMO went onto the longer 36-foot length, there again could not have been a greater difference. The S16 was long, lightweight and underpowered and, unlike its shorter S14 cousin, the company realised its mistake and placed 161 of the mechanically excellent S17s in service, as well as one S19, which was just a modified S17, and the three dual-purpose S21As.

The last three BMMO-built classes were another mixed bag, with the luxury S21s and S22s being as good as any other vehicles of their type in the country, while the final S23s were generally poorly constructed, with bodywork being increasingly put together using whatever parts were available or what was left in the parts bin in Central Works.

The original design philosophy of building advanced, reliable and lightweight buses had been at the heart of the decision to manufacture their own vehicles in 1923 after a number of small Garford chassis, which were made in Ohio, USA, were purchased in 1922, and BMMO continued with these values until production ended in 1970.